POCKET
GOOD
GUIDES

THE BEST
DOG
FRIENDLY
PUBS, HOTELS
AND B&Bs

THE BEST DOG FRIENDLY PUBS, HOTELS AND B&Bs

POCKET GOOD GUIDES

EDITED BY ALISDAIR AIRD

DEPUTY EDITOR FIONA STAPLEY

ASSOCIATE EDITORS: ELIZABETH ADLINGTON, KAREN FICK

EBURY PRESS

First published in Great Britain in 2003
Ebury Press
Random House
20 Vauxhall Bridge Road
London SW1 2SA

10 9 8 7 6 5 4 3 2 1

© Random House Group Ltd 2003

Alisdair Aird has asserted his moral right to be identified as the author of this
work under the Copyright, Designs and Patents Act 1988.

All rights reserved. No part of this publication may be reproduced, stored in a
retrieval system, or transmitted in any form or by any means, electronic,
mechanical, photocopying, recording or otherwise, without prior permission
from the copyright owners.

Random House Australia (Pty) Limited
20 Alfred Street, Milsons Point
Sydney
New South Wales 2061, Australia

Random House New Zealand Limited
18 Poland Road, Glenfield, Auckland 10
New Zealand

Random House South Africa (Pty) Limited
Endulini, 5A Jubilee Road
Parktown 2193
South Africa

Random House UK Limited Reg. No. 954009

www.randomhouse.co.uk

A CIP catalogue record for this book is available from the British Library

ISBN 0091889049

Papers used by Ebury Press are natural, recyclable products made from wood
grown in sustainable forests

Typeset by Textype, Cambridge
Cover design by Nim Design
Front cover image © ImageBank
Printed and bound in Denmark by Nørhaven Paperback A/S, Viborg

Introduction

The best dog friendly pubs, hotels and B&Bs

The Good Guides team, responsible for the best-selling *Good Pub Guide* and *Good Britain Guide* have used their comprehensive database – backed up by 45,000 reports from readers and their own anonymous inspections – to bring you a hand-picked list of over 600 places to eat and stay where the proprietors have said dogs are welcome. In the *Good Pub Guide*, where 60% of all the 1,318 main entries allow dogs inside, the descriptions of the entries are far more detailed; these short recommendations will give you a taster.

These hotels, inns and pubs, B&Bs and farms in villages or lovely countryside have been chosen not only because dogs are allowed in at least some part of the establishment, but also because they are in (or very close to) particularly good areas for walks – perhaps in open country, by interesting rivers or on the coast. So whether you want a day out with your dog to include an enjoyable meal and a fine walk or if you are planning a holiday away from home, there are plenty of friendly places for you to chose from where you will all be welcomed.

To contact the Pocket Good Guides team,
please write to

Pocket Good Guides
Freepost TN1 569
Wadhurst
E. Sussex
TN5 7BR

or check out
www.goodguides.co.uk

Britain's best areas for dogs

In some areas, pub landlords and landladies are so used to customers' dogs that it's really easy to find a good pub where you can pop in for a bar lunch, and bring your dog in, too. This year we have done a special survey of all the main entries in our companion *The Good Pub Guide 2003*, to find out which allow dogs into at least some part of the pub.

The Isle of Wight stands out, with virtually 100% acceptance of dogs in its good pubs. Also excellent for dog lovers in search of a bar lunch are Kent, Sussex, Hampshire and Devon, with at least nine out of ten good pubs there allowing dogs inside.

It's no surprise to find that big city pubs are relatively unwelcoming to dogs. Only about one in four in London allows them. Other areas in which the pub-loving dog tends to have a rather lean time are Staffordshire, Worcestershire and Lincolnshire – one in three pubs or less.

We have scoured all areas of Great Britain for places to stay in with dogs, where there are plenty of worthwhile walks. Some parts really stand out. The areas for discriminating dogs to put at the top of their holiday wish-list are the Lake District, Yorkshire, Devon, Wiltshire, Scotland and Wales. All these are rich in really nice places to stay in, and abound in interesting walks.

Contents

Factual details

We list opening hours for pubs, whether they have a restaurant, and if they offer bar food. Standard food times in pubs is from 12–2, 7–9 Monday to Saturday (food service often stops a bit earlier on Sundays). If food times are significantly different to this we list the times. We note days when we know pubs do not do food or are closed altogether but suggest you should play safe on Sundays and check first before planning an expedition that depends on getting a meal there. Pubs that are out-of-the-way may cut down on cooking times if they're quiet, which they tend to be except at holiday times.

For hotel and B&B accommodation, the price we show is the total for two people sharing a double or twin-bedded room with its own bathroom for one night in high season. It includes a full English breakfast, VAT and any automatic service charge that we know about. We say if dinner is included in this total price which it may be for some of the more remote places.

An asterisk beside the price means that the establishment concerned assured us that the price would hold until the end of summer 2003. Many establishments were unable to give us this assurance, so it would be prudent to allow for an increase of around 5% by then.

A few hotels will do a bargain break price at weekends even if you're staying for just one night. If so, that's the price we give, and we show this with a w beside the price. Many more hotels have very good value short break prices, especially out of season, so it's always worth asking.

If we know that the back rooms are the quietest or the front ones have the best views or the ones in the new extension are more spacious then we say so.

We always mention a restaurant if we know there is one and we commend food if we have information supporting a positive recommendation. Many B&Bs will recommend nearby pubs for evening meals if they do not offer dinner.

BEDFORDSHIRE

Dog Friendly Hotels and B&Bs

FLITWICK Flitwick Manor *Church Rd, Flitwick, Bedford, Bedfordshire MK45 IAE (01525) 712242* **£218**, plus special breaks; 17 thoughtfully decorated rms. 17th-c country house surrounded by interesting gardens, with log fire in entrance hall, comfortable lounge and library, and smart restaurant with fine French wines and imaginative food using home-grown and local produce; tennis, putting, croquet; children over 12 in evening restaurant; dogs welcome in bedrooms

SANDY Highfield Farm *Tempsford Rd, Sandy, Bedfordshire SG19 2AQ (01767) 682332* **£55**; 10 rms (2 in former stables). Neatly kept whitewashed house (no smoking) set well away from A1 and surrounded by attractive arable farmland with plenty of room for children to run around; warmly friendly, helpful owner, open fire in comfortable sitting room, and communal breakfasts in pleasant dining room; disabled access; dogs welcome in bedrooms

Dog Friendly Pubs

LINSLADE
Globe *Globe Lane, off Stoke Road (A4146) nr bridge; outside Linslade proper, just before you get to the town sign*
19th-c pub below Grand Union Canal embankment, cosy and attractive beamed and flagstoned rooms with log and coal fires, straightforward bar food, efficient service, plenty of towpath and other outdoor tables, well equipped play area;

the Cross Bucks Way leads off from just along the canal
*Greene King ~ Manager Nick Hughes ~ Real ale ~ Bar food (not
Sun evening in winter) ~ Restaurant ~ (01525) 373338 ~
Children in eating area of bar and restaurant ~ Dogs allowed in
bar ~ Open 11–11; 12–10.30 Sun*

BERKSHIRE

Dog Friendly Hotels and B&Bs

HUNGERFORD Marshgate Cottage *Marsh Lane,
Hungerford, Berkshire RG17 0QN (01488) 682307* **£55***; 10
individually decorated rms. Family-run little hotel backing on
to Kennet & Avon Canal, with residents' lounge and bar,
super breakfasts, a friendly atmosphere, and seats
overlooking water and marsh, and in sheltered courtyard;
plenty to see nearby; disabled access; dogs by arrangement

Dog Friendly Pubs

ALDWORTH
Bell *A329 Reading–Wallingford; left on to B4009 at Streatley*
Unchanging 14th-c country pub, run by the same charming
family for over 200 years; a huge favourite with walkers,
cyclists and locals (the Ridgeway is nearby), very traditional
layout and atmosphere, food confined to exceptionally good
value hot crusty filled rolls and winter home-made soup;
particularly well kept real ales, good house wines, lovely
old-fashioned garden

Free house ~ Licensee H E Macaulay ~ Real ale ~ Bar food (11–2.45, 6–10.45; 12–2.45, 7–10.15 Sun) ~ No credit cards ~ (01635) 578272 ~ Children must be well behaved ~ Dogs welcome ~ Open 11–3, 6–11; 12–3, 7–10.30 Sun; closed Mon exc bank hols

WALTHAM ST LAWRENCE
Bell In village centre

Timbered pub in pretty village setting, beams, panelling and log fire, plans for their own micro-brewery, generous tasty food, tables outside

Free house ~ Licensee I F Glenister ~ Real ale ~ Bar food (not Sun evening) ~ (0118) 934 1788 ~ Children in eating area of bar, in restaurant and family room ~ Dogs welcome ~ Open 12–3, 5–11; 12–11 Sat; 12–10.30 Sun

BUCKINGHAMSHIRE

Dog Friendly Hotels and B&Bs

AYLESBURY Hartwell House Oxford Rd, Aylesbury, Buckinghamshire HP17 8NL (01296) 747444 **£235**, plus special breaks; 46 rms, some huge and well equipped, others with four-posters and fine panelling, inc ten secluded suites in restored 18th-c stables with private garden and statues. Elegant Grade I listed building with Jacobean and Georgian façades, wonderful decorative plasterwork and panelling, fine paintings and antiques, a marvellous Gothic central staircase, splendid morning room, and library, exceptional service, pricey wines, and excellent food; 90 acres of parkland with ruined church, lake and statues, and spa with indoor swimming pool, saunas, gym and beauty rooms, and informal restaurant; croquet, fishing; children over 8; good disabled access; dogs in Hartwell Court

TAPLOW Cliveden *Taplow, Maidenhead, Berkshire SL6 0JF (01628) 668561* **£250** (plus £7 each paid to National Trust), plus special breaks; 39 luxurious, individual rms with maid unpacking service and a butler's tray. Superb Grade I listed stately home with gracious, comfortable public rooms, fine paintings, tapestries and armour, and a surprisingly unstuffy atmosphere; lovely views over the magnificent NT Thames-side parkland and formal gardens (open to the public); imaginative food in the two no smoking restaurants with lighter meals in the conservatory, friendly breakfasts around a huge table, and impeccable staff; pavilion with swimming pool, gym, etc; tennis, squash, croquet, riding, coarse fishing, a new golf course 5 minutes away reached by chauffeur-driven car, and boats for river trips; they are kind to children; good disabled access; dogs welcome away from eating areas

WINSLOW Bell *Market Sq, Winslow, Buckingham, Buckinghamshire MK18 3AB (01296) 714091* **£64**; 43 rms. Carefully refurbished and elegant black and white timbered inn with beams and open fires, plush hotel bar, all-day coffee lounge, enjoyable bar food, and good lunchtime and evening carvery in restaurant; disabled access; dogs welcome in bedrooms

Dog Friendly Pubs

FRIETH
Prince Albert *Village signposted off B482 in Lane End; turn right towards Fingest just before village*

Old-fashioned two-room cottagey country pub with low black beams, high-backed settles, big log fires, good bar food, particularly well kept beers, warm welcoming licensees; nice informal side garden, plenty of nearby walks
Brakspears ~ Tenant Steve Anderson ~ Real ale ~ Bar food (12–3, 6–9.30) ~ No credit cards ~ (01494) 881683 ~ Children welcome ~ Dogs welcome ~ Open 11.30–3.30, 5.30–11; 12–11 Sat; 12–10.30 Sun

TURVILLE
Bull & Butcher *Valley road off A4155 Henley–Marlow at Mill End, past Hambleden and Skirmett*
Black and white timbered pub in a lovely Chilterns valley, two low-beamed rooms with a well and an inglenook, good bar food, beer and wine; tables out by fruit trees in attractive garden
Brakspears ~ Tenant Nicholas Abbott ~ Real ale ~ Bar food (12–2.30(4 Sun and bank hols), 7–9.45; not Sun evening/bank hols) ~ Restaurant ~ (01491) 638283 ~ Children welcome ~ Dogs welcome ~ Open 11–3, 6(6.30 Sat)–11; 12–5, 7–10.30 Sun

CAMBRIDGESHIRE

Dog Friendly Hotels and B&Bs

DUXFORD Duxford Lodge *Ickleton Rd, Duxford, Cambridge CB2 4RU (01223) 836444* **£115***; 15 good-sized, warm rms, 2 with four-posters. Carefully run late Victorian hotel in an acre of neatly kept landscaped gardens, with a welcoming, relaxed atmosphere, individually chosen modern paintings and prints, a restful little lounge, decent wines, enjoyable modern cooking in the airy newly refurbished no smoking restaurant, and good breakfasts; cl 24 Dec–1 Jan; dogs welcome in bedrooms

ELY Lamb *2 Lynn Rd, Ely, Cambridgeshire CB7 4EJ (01353) 663574* **£95***; 32 comfortable rms. Pleasant, neatly kept old coaching inn nr the cathedral, with two smart bars, enjoyable food in an attractive restaurant, very friendly staff, and good car parking; dogs welcome in bedrooms

HUNTINGDON Old Bridge *1 High St, Huntingdon, Cambridgeshire PE18 6TQ (01480) 452681* **£145***, plus wknd breaks; 24 excellent rms with CD stereos and power showers. Creeper-covered Georgian hotel with pretty lounge, log fire in panelled bar, imaginative British cooking and extensive wine list in the no smoking restaurant and less formal lunchtime room (nice murals), and quick courteous service; riverside gardens; partial disabled access; dogs welcome in bedrooms

SIX MILE BOTTOM Swynford Paddocks *Six Mile Bottom, Newmarket, Cambridgeshire CB8 0UE (01638) 570234* **£110**; 15 individually furnished rms with good bthrms. Gabled country house in neat grounds overlooking stud paddocks; carefully furnished, newly refurbished rooms with fresh flowers and log fires, a new conservatory Garden Room, a relaxed atmosphere, good food, and friendly service; tennis, putting, and croquet; disabled access; dogs welcome in bedrooms

WANSFORD Haycock *London Rd, Wansford, Peterborough, Cambridgeshire PE8 6JA (01780) 782223* **£110**, plus special breaks; 50 attractively decorated rms. Old-fashioned golden stone inn with relaxed, comfortable, carefully furnished lounges and pubby bar; pretty lunchtime café, smart restaurant with good food, excellent wines and efficient friendly service; garden with boules, fishing and cricket; disabled access. The little village it dominates is attractive, with a fine bridge over the Nene, and a good antiques shop; dogs welcome in bedrooms

CHESHIRE

Dog Friendly Hotels and B&Bs

BEESTON Wild Boar Hotel *Whitchurch Rd, Beeston, Tarporley, Cheshire CW6 9NW (01829) 260309* **£105.75**, plus special breaks; 37 rms with appealing touches such as fresh fruit. Striking timbered 17th-c former hunting lodge, much extended over the years, with relaxed and comfortable bars and lounges, enjoyable bar meals and formal beamed restaurant, and good helpful service; disabled access; dogs in ground floor bedrooms only

BICKLEY MOSS Cholmondeley Arms *Cholmondeley, Malpas, Cheshire SY14 8HN (01829) 720300* **£60***, plus special breaks; 2 rms with bath, 4 with showers. Airy converted Victorian schoolhouse close to castle and gardens (famously, Cholmondeley is pronounced 'Chumley'), with lots of atmosphere, very friendly staff, interesting furnishings, open fire, excellent imaginative bar food, and very good choice of wines; disabled access; dogs welcome anywhere

CHESTER Castle House *23 Castle St, Chester CH1 2DS (01244) 350354* **£50***, plus special breaks; 5 comfortable rms, 3 with own bthrm. Small carefully preserved 16th-c guest house in the middle of the city, with helpful friendly owners, and fine breakfasts; dogs welcome in bedrooms

COTEBROOK Alvanley Arms *Cotebrook, Tarporley, Cheshire CW6 9DS (01829) 760200* **£60**; 7 rms. Handsome 400-year-old sandstone inn with pleasant beamed rooms (three areas are no smoking), big open fire, a chintzy little hall, shire horse décor (pictures, photographs, horseshoes, horse brasses, harness and bridles), generous helpings of good food, and a garden with lake and trout; shire horse stud next door opening Easter 2002; dogs welcome in bedrooms

FULLERS MOOR Frogg Manor *Nantwich Rd, Broxton, Chester CH3 9JH (01829) 782629* **£107**, plus special breaks; 7 lavishly decorated rms with thoughtful extras. Enjoyably eccentric Georgian manor house full of ornamental frogs and antique furniture, open fires and ornate dried-flower arrangements, a restful upstairs sitting room, cosy little bar, a large collection of 30s/40s records, and good English cooking in elegant dining room which leads to conservatory overlooking the gardens; disabled access; dogs welcome in bedrooms

HOOLE Hoole Hall *Warrington Rd, Hoole, Chester, Cheshire CH2 3PD (01244) 408800* **£133.75**, plus special breaks; 97 well equipped rms, some no smoking. Extended and attractively refurbished 18th-c hall with five acres of gardens, good food in two restaurants, and friendly service; good disabled access; dogs welcome in bedrooms

KNUTSFORD Longview *51–55 Manchester Rd, Knutsford, Cheshire WA16 0LX (01565) 632119* **£69.50**w; 26 rms. Friendly Victorian hotel with attractive period and repro-duction furnishings, open fires in original fireplaces, pleasant cellar bar, ornate restaurant, and good well presented food; cl Christmas–mid-Jan; dogs welcome in bedrooms

MACCLESFIELD Sutton Hall Hotel *Bullocks Lane, Sutton, Macclesfield, Cheshire SK11 0HE (01260) 253211* **£90**; 9 marvellous rms. Welcoming and secluded historic baronial hall, full of character, with stylish rooms, high black beams, stone fireplaces, suits of armour and so forth, friendly service, and good food; can arrange clay shooting/golf/fishing; dogs welcome in bedrooms

MOBBERLEY Laburnum Cottage *Knutsford Rd, Mobberley, Knutsford, Cheshire WA16 7PU (01565) 872464* **£57**; 4 pretty rms. Neatly kept and friendly no smoking country guest house in an acre of landscaped garden; relaxed atmosphere in comfortable lounge with books, a sunny conservatory, and very good food; disabled access (with prior notice); dogs by arrangement

POTT SHRIGLEY Shrigley Hall *Shrigley Park, Pott Shrigley, Macclesfield, Cheshire SK10 5SB (01625) 575757* **£120**, plus special breaks; 150 smart well equipped rms, some with country views. In over 260 acres of parkland, this impressive country house has a splendid entrance hall with several elegant rooms leading off, enjoyable food in the orangery and restaurant, and good service from friendly staff; championship golf course, fishing, tennis, and leisure centre in former church building; plenty to do nearby; disabled access; dogs welcome in bedrooms

SANDBACH Old Hall *High St, Sandbach, Cheshire CW11 1AL (01270) 761221* **£70**, plus special breaks; 12 comfortable rms. Fine Jacobean timbered hotel with lots of original panelling and fireplaces, relaxing refurbished lounge, friendly welcome, and popular, newly refurbished restaurant; disabled access; dogs welcome

WHEELOCK Grove House *Mill Lane, Wheelock, Sandbach, Cheshire CW11 4RD (01270) 762582* **£60**; 8 rms with showers. Family-run Georgian restaurant-with-rooms, with relaxed homely atmosphere, quietly furnished lounge and restaurant, personal friendly service, and very good modern cooking in popular restaurant; plenty to do nearby; cl 22 Dec–3 Jan; dogs welcome in bedrooms

WORLESTON Rookery Hall *Main Rd, Worleston, Nantwich, Cheshire CW5 6DQ (01270) 610016* **£95**, plus special breaks; 45 individually decorated rms. Fine early 19th-c hotel in 38 acres of lovely parkland, with elegant lounges, log fires, intimate panelled restaurant with enjoyable food, and friendly service; disabled access; dogs in bedrooms in Coach House

Dog Friendly Pubs

BARTHOMLEY
White Lion *A mile from M6 junction 16; from the A500 towards Stoke-on-Trent, take B5078 Alsager road, then Barthomley signposted on left*
Lovely black and white thatched pub with timeless bar, inviting open fire, heavy oak beams, attractively moulded black panelling, latticed windows, and wobbly old tables; good value generous lunchtime bar food, friendly efficient staff, tables out on cobbles, delightful village; you can rent the cottage behind the pub.
Burtonwood ~ Tenant Terence Cartwright ~ Real ale ~ Bar food (lunchtime only, not Thurs) ~ (01270) 882242 ~ Children welcome away from public bar ~ Dogs welcome ~ Open 11.30–11(5–11 only Thurs); 12–10.30 Sun

BELL O' TH' HILL
Blue Bell *Signposted just off A41 N of Whitchurch*
Easy-going very heavily beamed 14th-c country local, and the welcoming Californian landlord positively encourages you to bring your pets; very good value home-made bar food, well kept real ales, tables outside; ask about walks – there's a nice one to the pub at Willey Moor Lock
Free house ~ Licensees Pat and Lydia Gage ~ Real ale ~ Bar food (12–2, 6–9) ~ Restaurant ~ No credit cards ~ (01948) 662172 ~ Children welcome ~ Dogs welcome ~ Open 12–3, 6–11(7–11 Sun)

WRENBURY
Dusty Miller *Village signposted from A530 Nantwich–Whitchurch*
Former 19th-c mill overlooking Shropshire Union Canal through tall glazed arches, banquettes around rustic tables in comfortably modern main bar, popular hearty food using local ingredients, pleasant waterside picnic-sets
Robinsons ~ Tenant Mark Sumner ~ Real ale ~ Bar food (not Mon in winter) ~ Restaurant ~ (01270) 780537 ~ Children in restaurant ~ Dogs allowed in bar ~ Open 11.30–3 (not Mon), 6.30–11; 12–3, 7–10.30 Sun

CORNWALL

Dog Friendly Hotels and B&Bs

CARNE BEACH Nare Hotel *Carne Beach, Veryan, Truro, Cornwall TR2 5PF (01872) 501279* **£252** inc afternoon tea, plus special breaks; 36 lovely rms to suit all tastes – some stylish ones overlook garden and out to sea. Attractively decorated and furnished hotel in magnificent clifftop position with secluded gardens, outdoor and indoor swimming pools, tennis, sailboarding, and fishing; antiques, fresh flowers and log fires in the airy, spacious day rooms, very good food in two restaurants (one is new this year, with a more relaxed atmosphere), wonderful breakfasts, and run by staff who really care; ideal for quiet family hols, with safe sandy beach below; disabled access; dogs welcome in bedrooms

CONSTANTINE BAY Treglos Hotel *Constantine Bay, Padstow, Cornwall PL28 8JH (01841) 520727* **£95**, plus special breaks; 42 light rms, some with balcony. Quiet and relaxed hotel close to good sandy beach, and in the same family for 30 years; comfortable traditional furnishings, log fires, good food, friendly helpful staff, sheltered garden plus playground and adventure equipment, indoor swimming pool, table tennis, table football, and pool table, and children's playroom with electronic games; lovely nearby walks; self-catering apartments; cl mid Nov–mid-Mar; children over 7 in restaurant; disabled access; dogs welcome in bedrooms

CRANTOCK Crantock Bay Hotel *West Pentire, Crantock, Newquay, Cornwall TR8 5SE (01637) 830229* **£73***, plus special breaks; 33 comfortable rms, most with coastal views. In a lovely setting on the West Pentire headland, facing the Atlantic and a huge sheltered sandy beach, this relaxed and informal hotel has been run by the same friendly family for 50 years; four acres of grounds, an indoor swimming pool, toddlers' pool, sauna and exercise room, all weather tennis court, a putting course, and children's play area; two lounges, bar lounge and restaurant, enjoyable food using local produce, and nice afternoon teas; cl early Nov–end Jan; families most welcome; lots to do nearby; disabled access and facilities; dogs welcome away from public rooms

FALMOUTH Penmere Manor *Mongleath Rd, Falmouth, Cornwall TR11 4PN* (01326) 211411 **£102**, plus special breaks; 37 spacious rms. Run by the same owners for 29 years, this quietly set Georgian manor has five acres of subtropical gardens and woodland, heated outdoor swimming pool, giant chess, croquet, and leisure centre with indoor swimming pool, gym, sauna, and woodland fitness trail; particularly helpful friendly staff, an evening pianist, and enjoyable food in restaurant and informal bar; cl 24–27 Dec; dogs welcome in bedrooms

FOWEY Fowey Hall *Fowey, Cornwall PL23 1ET* (01726) 833866 **£160**; 24 rms inc 11 suites and 4 pairs of interconnecting rms. Fine Gothic-style mansion in five acres of grounds overlooking the harbour and run along the same lines as their other hotels – Woolley Grange, Bradford-on-Avon, Moonfleet Manor at Fleet, and Old Bell, Malmesbury; marble fireplaces, baroque plasterwork, panelling, antiques, big potted plants, two enjoyable restaurants, marvellous facilities for children inc supervised nursery, and covered swimming pool, croquet, and badminton; dogs welcome away from eating areas

GERRANS BAY Pendower Beach House *Ruan High Lanes, Truro, Cornwall TR2 5LW* (01872) 501241 **£164** inc dinner, plus special breaks; 14 rms. Family-run hotel dating back to 16th c in eight acres by lovely sandy beach, with superb sea and coastal views, and plenty of seats on sunny terrace; a relaxed, friendly atmosphere in attractive and comfortable rooms, good food in cosy restaurant (super fresh local fish and shellfish), and tennis court; cl Nov–Feb; disabled access; dogs welcome in bedrooms

GILLAN Tregildry *Gillan, Manaccan, Helston, Cornwall TR12 6HG* (01326) 231378 **£144*** inc dinner, plus special breaks; 10 attractive rms with fine views over Falmouth Bay. Elegantly furnished hotel in four acres of grounds with private access to the cove below; spacious comfortable lounges, fresh flowers, books and magazines, a restful atmosphere, very good food in attractive restaurant, enjoyable breakfasts, and kind, courteous service; cl Nov–Feb; children over 8; dogs welcome in bedrooms

LISKEARD Well House *St Keyne, Liskeard, Cornwall PL14 4RN* (01579) 342001 **£110**, plus special breaks; 9 individually designed rms with fine views. Light and airy Victorian country house, recently redecorated, with warm, friendly owners, courteous staff, comfortable drawing room, cosy little bar, and particularly good food and fine wines in dining room overlooking terrace and lawns; three acres of gardens with hard tennis court, swimming pool and croquet lawn; children over 8 in evening restaurant; dogs welcome in bedrooms

LOOE Talland Bay Hotel *Porthallow, Looe, Cornwall PL13 2JB* (01503) 272667 **£110**, plus special breaks; 22 charming rms with sea or country views. Down a little lane between Looe and Polperro, this restful partly 16th-c country house has lovely subtropical gardens just above the sea; comfortable drawing room with log fire, smaller lounge with library, fresh flowers, courteous service, good food in pretty oak-panelled dining room, and pleasant afternoon teas; heated outdoor swimming pool, putting, croquet; cl Jan; children over 5 in evening restaurant (high tea for younger ones); dogs welcome in bedrooms

MAWNAN SMITH Meudon Hotel *Mawnan Smith, Falmouth, Cornwall TR11 5HT (01326) 250541* **£200** inc dinner, plus special breaks; 29 well equipped comfortable rms in separate wing. Run by the same caring family for over 36 years, this is an old stone mansion with a newer wing, in beautiful subtropical gardens laid out 200 years ago by R W Fox; fine views from the dining room, comfortable lounge with log fire and fresh flowers, good English cooking, and old-fashioned standards of service; cl 3–31 Jan; disabled access; dogs welcome in bedrooms

MITHIAN Rose-in-Vale Country House Hotel *Mithian, St Agnes, Cornwall TR5 0QD (01872) 552202* **£99**, plus special breaks; 18 pretty rms inc 2 suites. Secluded and quietly set Georgian house in four acres of neatly kept gardens, with comfortable spacious day rooms, a friendly atmosphere, helpful, long-standing local staff, and good food in enlarged dining room; ducks on ponds, a trout steam, outdoor swimming pool, badminton, and croquet, plus a sauna and solarium; children over 7 in evening in public rooms and restaurant (high tea for smaller ones); cl Jan–Feb; disabled access; dogs welcome in bedrooms

MULLION Meaver Farm *Meaver Rd, Mullion, Helston, Cornwall TR12 7DN (01326) 240128* **£50**, plus special breaks; 3 individual rms with super bthrms. 17th-c stone farmhouse (no longer a working farm), with good Aga-cooked breakfasts in beamed kitchen, log fire, plants and antiques in sitting room, and friendly helpful owners; dogs welcome

MULLION Polurrian Hotel *Mullion, Helston, Cornwall TR12 7EN (01326) 240421* **£130** inc dinner, plus special breaks; 39 rms, some with memorable sea view. White clifftop hotel in lovely gardens with path down to sheltered private cove below, a restful atmosphere in the comfortable lounges and bright cocktail bar, fresh flowers, good food using fresh local ingredients (pianist and sea views in the dining room), enjoyable breakfasts, leisure club with heated swimming pool, and heated outdoor pool, badminton, tennis, mini-golf, squash and croquet; particularly good for families; disabled access; dogs welcome

PENZANCE Abbey Hotel *Abbey St, Penzance, Cornwall TR18 4AR* (01736) 366906 **£105**, plus winter breaks; 7 charming rms. Stylish little 17th-c house close to harbour with marvellous views, a relaxed atmosphere in comfortable drawing room full of flowers, fine paintings and antiques, a good set menu in small restaurant, and pretty garden; cl 1 wk Christmas; children over 7 in dining room; dogs welcome in bedrooms

PENZANCE Georgian House Hotel *20 Chapel Street, Penzance, Cornwall TR18 4AW* (01736) 365664 **£46**; 11 comfortable rms, most with own bthrm. Warmly friendly little hotel, once the home of the Mayor of Penzance and close to the harbour and shopping centre, with helpful owner and staff, very good breakfasts in attractive dining room, reading lounge, and private parking; cl Christmas–mid-Jan; dogs welcome in bedrooms

PORT ISAAC Port Gaverne Hotel *Port Gaverne, Port Isaac, Cornwall PL29 3SQ* (01208) 880244 **£80**, plus special breaks; 15 comfortable rms. Lovely place to stay and an excellent base for area (dramatic coves, good clifftop walks, and lots of birds); big log fires in well kept bars, relaxed lounges, decent bar food, good restaurant food, and fine wines; also, restored 18th-c self-catering cottages; cl 5 Jan–12 Feb; children over 7 in restaurant; dogs anywhere except dining room

RUAN HIGH LANES Crugsillick Manor *Ruan High Lanes, Truro, Cornwall TR2 5LJ (01872) 501214* **£80**, plus special breaks; 3 rms. One of the loveliest houses in Cornwall, this Queen Anne manor is extended from a pre-Elizabethan farmhouse and surrounded by a big quiet garden with wooded valley views; log fire in drawing room with Napoleonic ceiling, candlelit dinners in 17th-c dining room using home-grown produce where possible, fine breakfasts, and charming owners; self-catering cottages in grounds – excellent disabled access, and children welcome (but must be over 12 in main house); house cl Christmas (self-catering open then); dogs anywhere in cottages, not in bedrooms in house

SALTASH Erth Barton *Elmgate, Saltash, Cornwall PL12 4QY (01752) 842127* **£70**; 3 rms. Lovely old manor house with its own chapel, peaceful rooms with lots of books, pictures and big fireplaces, good enjoyable food, bird-watching in the surrounding estuaries, and riding (you can bring your own horse); children over 12; dogs welcome anywhere

SENNEN Land's End Hotel *Sennen, Penzance, Cornwall TR19 7AA (01736) 871844* **£130**, plus special breaks; 33 elegant airy rms, many with splendid sea views. Comfortable hotel right on the cliff top with fine sea views, good food in attractive conservatory-style restaurant, elegant seating areas, informal bar with lots of malt whiskies, and helpful staff; lots to do nearby; cl end Oct–1 Mar; dogs welcome in bedrooms

ST IVES Garrack *Burthallan Lane, St Ives, Cornwall TR26 3AA (01736) 796199* **£131***, plus winter breaks; 20 rms, some in more modern wing. Friendly hotel in two acres of gardens with wonderful sea views, cosy lounges with antiques, books and open fires, a family room, good food inc fresh shellfish, helpful staff, and indoor leisure centre; disabled access; dogs welcome in bedrooms

ST MAWES Rising Sun *The Square, St Mawes, Truro, Cornwall TR2 5DJ* (01326) 270233 **£64.50***; 8 rms. Small attractive hotel in popular picturesque waterside village, with harbour views, large comfortable lounge bar area, airy conservatory, charming terrace; dogs welcome in bedrooms

TREVAUNANCE COVE Driftwood Spars *Trevaunance Cove, St Agnes, Cornwall TR5 0RT* (01872) 552428 **£68**; 15 attractive, comfortable bdrms, some with sea view, 8 in separate building. Friendly family-owned hotel dating from the 17th c and just up the road from the beach and dramatic cove; woodburner in comfortable lounge, main bar with large open fire, upstairs gallery, beamed ceilings, helpful staff, and enjoyable food; live music wknds; cl 25 Dec; dogs welcome anywhere

ISLES OF SCILLY

Dog Friendly Hotels and B&Bs

PELISTRY BAY Carnwethers Country House *Carnwethers, Pelistry Bay, St Mary's, Isles of Scilly TR21 0NX* (01720) 422415 **£120*** inc dinner – good value weekly terms, too; 9 rms. Well run no smoking country guesthouse nr very fine beach, with an acre of lovely gardens, heated swimming pool, and croquet, lounge with helpful books about the islands, well stocked bar, good freshly cooked set

4-course dinner using local produce served at 6.30pm, sound wine list, and games room with pool table and table tennis; sauna; lots of coastal walks; cl Oct–mid Apr; children over 10; dogs welcome in bedrooms

ST AGNES Coastguards *St Agnes, Isles of Scilly, TR22 0PL* *(01720) 422373* **£69** inc dinner; 3 rms in separate cottages, with views of the sea. Peacefully set former coastguard cottages with open fire, interesting artefacts, and sea views in the sitting room, enjoyable homely dinners and breakfasts, friendly, helpful owners, and big garden; no smoking; cl Nov–Mar; children over 12; dogs welcome in bedrooms

ST MARTIN'S St Martin's on the Isle *Lower Town, St Martin's, Isles of Scilly TR25 0QW (01720) 422092* **£170**, plus special breaks. 30 attractively decorated rms, most with fine sea views. Welcomed by the friendly manager as you step off the boat, you find this stone-built hotel set idyllically on a white sand beach, with stunning sunsets; comfortable, light and airy split-level bar-lounge with doors opening on to the terrace, lovely flower arrangements, genuinely friendly professional staff, sophisticated food in main restaurant (lighter lunches in the bar), and a fine wine list; they are particularly kind to children with buckets and spades to borrow, videos, and high tea for under-12s (they must be 12 or over in evening restaurant); fine walks (the island is car free), launch trips to other islands, and good bird-watching; small swimming pool; cl Nov–Feb; disabled access; dogs welcome in bedrooms

Dog Friendly Pubs

MANACCAN
New Inn *Down hill signed to Gillan and St Keverne*
Comfortably olde-worlde thatched village pub with beamed double-room bar, friendly landlady and courteous staff, good bar food inc great choice of lunchtime sandwiches, more elaborate evening dishes; picnic-sets in rose-filled garden, lovely setting in pretty waterside village
Pubmaster ~ Tenant Penny Williams ~ Real ale ~ Bar food (12–2.30, 6.30–9.30) ~ (01326) 231323 ~ Children welcome ~ Dogs welcome ~ Open 12–3, 6–11; 12–3, 7–10.30 Sun

ST AGNES
Turks Head *The Quay*
Beautifully placed cottagey pub with maritime bric-a-brac in simple and friendly pine-panelled bar, real ales, decent food and drinks, some evening barbecues, cats called Taggart and Lacey, and a collie called Tess, wonderful sea views from tables outside – you can sit right on the shore; good bedrooms
Free house ~ Licensees John and Pauline Dart ~ Real ale ~ Bar food (12–2.30, 6.30–9) ~ (01720) 422434 ~ Children welcome if well behaved ~ Dogs allowed in bar ~ Open 11–11; 12–11 Sun; best to phone for limited opening hours in winter ~ Bedrooms: 1/£57B

ST MAWGAN
Falcon *NE of Newquay, off B3276 or A3059*
Neat, friendly and comfortable, with big antique coaching prints, a log fire, good generous interesting food, and efficient service; pretty cobbled courtyard, peaceful garden with play equipment, comfortable bedrooms and hearty breakfasts
St Austell ~ Tenant Andy Banks ~ Real ale ~ Bar food ~ Restaurant ~ (01637) 860225 ~ Children in restaurant ~ Dogs

welcome ~ Open 11–3, 6–11; 12–3, 7–10.30 Sun ~ Bedrooms:
£21/£50(£64S)
TRESCO
New Inn *New Grimsby; Isles of Scilly*
Chatty locals' bar and a bigger main bar, some comfortable
old sofas, boat stuff, farmhouse chairs and tables, cheerful
dining extension, well liked bar food served by friendly staff,
good Cornish and Scillonian beers and interesting wines;
teak furniture out on terrace, comfortable bedrooms (price
includes dinner)
Free house ~ Licensee Robin Lawson ~ Real ale ~ Bar food (all
day) ~ Restaurant ~ (01720) 423006 ~ Children welcome ~
Dogs allowed in bar ~ Irish band or rock and roll every 10 days
in winter ~ Open 11–11; 12–10.30 Sun; 12–2.30, 6–11 in
winter ~ Bedrooms: /£172B

CUMBRIA

Dog Friendly Hotels and B&Bs

ALSTON Lovelady Shield Country House *Nenthead*
Rd, Alston, Cumbria CA9 3LF (01434) 381203 **£180** inc dinner,
plus special breaks; 12 rms, though they hope to add 2 more.
In a lovely setting with River Nent running along bottom of
garden (tennis and croquet), this handsome country house
has a tranquil atmosphere, courteous staff, log fires in
comfortable rooms (no smoking in sitting room or
restaurant), and very good food inc fine breakfasts; children
over 7 in evening restaurant; dogs welcome in bedrooms
AMBLESIDE Wateredge Inn *Borrans Rd, Ambleside,*

Cumbria LA22 0EP (015394) 32332 **£90**, plus special breaks; 21 good comfortable, recently refurbished rms. Beautifully placed, warmly welcoming inn with neat gardens running down to Lake Windermere (embarkation point for cruising the lake); light airy bar (with fine views) and lounge, good meals in no smoking beamed dining area (more lovely views and candlelit at night), and excellent service; may cl 2 wks Jan; disabled access; dogs welcome in bedrooms

APPLEBY Appleby Manor *Roman Rd, Appleby, Cumbria CA16 6JB (01768) 351571* **£114***, plus special breaks; 30 well equipped rms in original house (the nicest), coach house annexe or modern wing. Very friendly family-run hotel with fine views over Appleby Castle and Eden Valley, log fires in two of the three comfortable lounges, relaxed bar with wide range of whiskies, excellent service, good interesting food in panelled restaurant, and leisure centre; enjoyed by families; cl 24–26 Dec; disabled access; dogs welcome in bedrooms

BARBON Barbon Inn *Barbon, Carnforth, Cumbria LA6 2LJ (015242) 76233* **£65**; 10 simple but comfortable rms, some with own bthrm. Small friendly village inn in quiet spot below fells, with relaxing bar, traditional lounge, good meals in candlelit dining room, and helpful service; dogs by prior arrangement

BASSENTHWAITE LAKE Pheasant *Bassenthwaite Lake, Cockermouth, Cumbria CA13 9YE (017687) 76234* **£130**, plus special breaks; 16 newly refurbished rms. Civilised hotel with delightfully old-fashioned pubby bar, restful lounges with open fire, antiques, fresh flowers and comfortable armchairs, and interesting gardens merging into surrounding fellside woodlands; cl 25 Dec; children over 8; disabled access; dogs in bar and in Garden Lodge bedrooms

BRAMPTON Farlam Hall *Hallbankgate, Brampton, Cumbria CA8 2NG (016977) 46234* **£250** inc dinner, plus special breaks; 12 comfortable rms. Charmingly Victorian (though parts are much older) and very civilised country house with log fires in spacious lounges, excellent attentive service, good 4-course dinner using fine china and silver, marvellous breakfasts, and peaceful spacious grounds with croquet lawn and small pretty lake; cl 25–30 Dec; children over 5; dogs welcome except in restaurant

BUTTERMERE Bridge *Buttermere, Cockermouth, Cumbria CA13 9UZ (017687) 70252* **£120** inc dinner, plus special breaks; 21 recently refurbished rms. Comfortable hotel surrounded by some of the best steep countryside in the county, with beamed bar, open fire and deep armchairs in sitting room, good food in bar and no smoking restaurant, real ales, decent malt whiskies, and a friendly atmosphere; self-catering also; children over 7 in dining room; dogs welcome in bedrooms

CASTERTON Pheasant *Casterton, Carnforth, Lancashire LA6 2RX (015242) 71230* **£76**, plus special breaks; 10 comfortable rms, most with countryside views, and several newly refurbished. Small civilised inn with pleasant atmosphere, good food in no smoking panelled dining room, cheerful staff, and small but sound wine list; cl 25–26 Dec; disabled access; dogs welcome

CROOK Wild Boar *Crook, Windermere, Cumbria LA23 3NF (015394) 45225* **£115**; 36 rms. Comfortable well run extended hotel with period furnishings and log fires in its ancient core, attentive service, and good food in no smoking dining room; free access to nearby leisure club and discounts on watersports; children's club at sister hotel, The Lowwood; dogs welcome

CROSBY ON EDEN Crosby Lodge *High Crosby, Crosby on Eden, Carlisle, Cumbria CA6 4QZ (01228) 573618* **£120***, plus special breaks; 11 spacious rms (2 in stable conversion). Imposing and carefully converted country house in attractive mature grounds, with comfortable and appealing individual furnishings, enjoyable home-made food using local produce in no smoking restaurant, friendly long-established owners, and nice surrounding countryside; cl Christmas and New Year; limited disabled access; dogs by arrangement

DENT Sportsmans *Cowgill, Dent, Sedbergh, Cumbria LA10 5RG (01539) 625282* **£47**, plus winter breaks; 6 rms with shared bthrm. Unassuming comfortable pub notable for its wonderful position in Dentdale by the River Dee overlooking the Settle–Carlisle railway, and walks in all directions; open log fires, real ales, and good value home-made food; dogs welcome in bedrooms

DERWENT WATER Hilton Keswick Lodore *Borrowdale, Keswick, Cumbria CA12 5UX (017687) 77285* **£143***, plus special breaks; 71 well equipped rms. Long-standing but well updated big holiday hotel with lots of facilities in 40 acres of lakeside gardens and woodlands, comfortable day rooms, elegant restaurant, leisure club, tennis and squash, outdoor swimming pool, and games room; particularly well organised for families, with NNEB nannies and so forth; self-catering house too; dogs welcome in bedrooms

DOCKRAY Royal *Dockray, Penrith, Cumbria CA11 0JY (017684) 82356* **£64**, plus special breaks; 10 rms. Friendly family-run hotel with open fires in big modernised open-plan bar, good value hearty meals, and well kept beers; in fine spot between hills and lake with walks from the doorstep; children must be well behaved; dogs welcome in bedrooms

ELTERWATER Britannia Inn *Elterwater, Ambleside, Cumbria LA22 9HP (015394) 37210* **£80**, plus special breaks; 9 rms. Simple charmingly traditional pub in fine surroundings opposite village green, with a happy friendly atmosphere (it does get very busy at peak times), hearty home cooking inc superb breakfast, comfortable no smoking lounge and bustling bar, real ales, and Sun evening quiz; fine walks all around; cl 25–26 Dec; dogs in bars and bedrooms

FAR SAWREY Sawrey *Far Sawrey, Ambleside, Cumbria LA22 0LQ (015394) 43425* **£63**, plus special breaks; 18 rms. Friendly hotel well placed at the foot of Claife Heights, with simple pubby and smarter bars, friendly staff, good straightforward food, and seats on pleasant lawn; cl Christmas; kind to children; partial disabled access; dogs welcome in bedrooms

GARRIGILL Ivy House *Garrigill, Alston, Cumbria CA9 3DU (01434) 382501* **£44***, plus special breaks; 3 rms. 17th-c farmhouse in fine scenery on Alston Moor, with a comfortable guest lounge, open fire and plenty of books, games and newspapers, helpful welcoming owners, and good breakfasts plus packed lunches and evening meals (which must be booked in advance); they also offer llama treks with instructions on how to handle and befriend them (children must be over 12 for this); dogs welcome

GRASMERE Swan *Keswick Rd, Grasmere, Ambleside, Cumbria LA22 9RF (015394) 35551* **£138**, plus special breaks; 38 rms, most with fine views. Smart and friendly 17th-c hotel in beautiful fell-foot surroundings, with beams and inglenooks, elegant no smoking dining room, enjoyable food, and attractive garden; lovely walks; partial disabled access; dogs anywhere except restaurant

GRIZEDALE Grizedale Lodge *Hawkshead Hill, Grizedale, Ambleside, Cumbria LA22 0QL (015394) 36532* **£75***, plus special breaks; 8 no smoking rms. Friendly, comfortable B&B hotel in the middle of the magnificent Grizedale Forest with lots of walks from the front door, lounge bar, and hearty breakfasts in attractive breakfast room; children over 5; disabled access; dogs welcome in bedrooms

HAWKSHEAD Highfield House *Hawkshead Hill, Ambleside, Cumbria LA22 0PN (015394) 36344* **£100***, plus winter breaks; 11 pretty rms. Welcoming Victorian country house in spacious woodland garden with fine views (good walks from the door), open fire in comfortable lounge, cosy bar, and enjoyable food inc packed lunches, children's high tea, and good breakfasts; cl Jan; dogs welcome in bedrooms

IREBY Overwater Hall *Ireby, Carlisle, Cumbria CA5 1HH (017687) 76566* **£100**, plus special breaks; 12 recently refurbished rms. Relaxed and friendly family-run hotel, partly castellated, in 18 acres of gardens and woodland, with log fire in elegant comfortable drawing room, good imaginative food in cosy dining room, and lots of walks; cl 2 wks from 3 Jan; children over 5 in restaurant (high tea 5 pm); partial disabled access; dogs in bedrooms and one lounge

KENDAL Low Jock Scar *Selside, Kendal, Cumbria LA8 9LE (01539) 823259* **£60***; 5 rms, most with own bthrm. Relaxed and friendly little country guesthouse in six acres of garden and woodland, with residents' lounge, and good home cooking (picnic lunches on request); no smoking; cl Nov–mid-Mar; children over 12; dogs welcome in bedrooms

LANGDALE Old Dungeon Ghyll *Great Langdale, Ambleside, Cumbria LA22 9JY (015394) 37272* **£78**, plus special breaks; 14 rms, some with shared bthrm. Friendly, simple and cosy walkers' and climbers' inn dramatically surrounded by fells, wonderful views and terrific walks; cosy residents' lounge and popular food – best to book for dinner if not a resident; cl Christmas; dogs welcome away from dining room

LORTON New House Farm *Lorton, Cockermouth, Cumbria CA13 9UU (01900) 85404* **£88**, plus special breaks; 5 rms with wonderful hillside views. Friendly no smoking 17th-c house (not a working farm) in 15 acres, with beams and rafters, flagstones, open fires, and three residents' lounges, very good food inc game and fish caught by owner, home-made scones and preserves, a thoughtful wine list – and lots of walks; children over 6; dogs welcome in bedrooms

MUNGRISDALE Mill Hotel *Mungrisdale, Penrith, Cumbria CA11 0XR (017687) 79659* **£85**; 9 rms, most with own bthrm. Very friendly small streamside hotel beautifully placed in lovely valley hamlet hidden away below Blencathra, with open fire in cosy and comfortable sitting room, good imaginative 5-course evening meals, and a small carefully chosen wine list; cl Nov–beginning Mar; they are kind to children; disabled access; dogs welcome in bedrooms

RYDAL WATER White Moss House *White Moss, Ambleside, Cumbria LA22 9SE (015394) 35295* **£138** inc dinner, plus special breaks; 6 thoughtfully furnished and comfortable little rms in main house plus separate cottage let as one unit with 2 rms. Bought by Wordsworth for his son, this attractive stripped-stone country house – set in charming mature grounds overlooking the lake – is a marvellously relaxing place to stay, with owners who have been there for over 20 years, a comfortable lounge, excellent fixed-price 5-course meals in pretty no smoking dining room, a fine wine list, and exemplary service; free fishing and free use of local leisure club; cl Dec–Jan; no toddlers; dogs in cottage

SEATOLLER Seatoller House *Borrowdale, Keswick, Cumbria CA12 5XN* (017687) 77218 **£59**; 10 spotless, comfortable rms. Friendly house-party atmosphere in 17th-c house that has been a guesthouse for over 100 yrs, with self-service drinks and board games in comfortable lounges (no TV), and good no-choice fixed-time hearty dinner (not Tues) served at two big oak tables; packed lunches; two acres of grounds and many walks from doorstep (house is at the foot of Honister Pass); cl end Nov–Mar; dogs welcome

TIRRIL Queens Head *Tirril, Penrith, Cumbria CA10 2JF* (01768) 863219 **£60***, plus special breaks; 7 lovely rms, most with own bthrm. Bustling very welcoming inn with flagstones and bare boards in the bar, spacious back restaurant (mostly no smoking), low beams, black panelling, inglenook fireplace and old-fashioned settles in older part, good interesting food inc snacks and OAP specials, and well kept real ales (inc their own brews); babies welcome but older children must be over 13; dogs welcome except in restaurant

WATERMILLOCK Leeming House *Watermillock, Ullswater, Penrith, Cumbria CA11 0JJ* (017684) 86622 **£148**, plus special breaks; 40 cosseting rms, many with beautiful views. Well run extended hotel in 20 acres of quiet lakeside grounds, with log fires in comfortable lounges, cosy panelled bar, fine food in lovely no smoking dining room, and good courteous service; boating and fishing; high teas for young children; good provision for disabled; dogs welcome in bedrooms

WATERMILLOCK Rampsbeck Country House
Watermillock, Penrith, Cumbria CA11 0LP (017684) 86442
£100, plus special breaks; 20 attractive rms, some with
balconies. 18th-c hotel in 18 acres by Lake Ullswater with
extensive lake frontage; open fire in the cosy sitting room,
French windows into the garden from the plush,
comfortable lounge, friendly attentive staff, and carefully
prepared food in the attractive dining room; croquet; lots
to do nearby; cl Jan–mid-Feb; children over 8 in dining rm;
dogs welcome in bedrooms

WINDERMERE Langdale Chase Hotel *Windermere,
Cumbria LA23 1LW* (015394) 32201 **£150**; 27 rms, many
with marvellous lake view. Welcoming family-run hotel in
lovely position on the edge of Lake Windermere with
water-skiing and bathing from the hotel jetty; tennis,
croquet, putting and rowing, afternoon tea on the terraces,
gracious oak-panelled rooms with antiques, paintings, fresh
flowers, open fires, very good food (huge breakfasts, too),
and friendly service; disabled access; dogs welcome

WITHERSLACK Old Vicarage *Witherslack, Grange-over-
Sands, Cumbria LA11 6RS* (015395) 52381 **£75** inc dinner,
plus special breaks; 14 individually decorated rms – some in
the modern Orchard House are more spacious and have
their own woodland terraces. Late Georgian vicarage in five
acres of peaceful gardens and woodland, with two
comfortable lounges, a log fire, good interesting food in
cosy restaurant inc home-made bread, cakes and preserves,
and hearty breakfasts; tennis and lots of surrounding walks;
dogs welcome in bedrooms

Dog Friendly Pubs

HESKET NEWMARKET
Old Crown *Village signposted off B5299 in Caldbeck*
Relaxed and unfussy local brewing its own good beers, enjoyable home cooking inc popular evening curries, coal fire and shelves of well thumbed books, friendly atmosphere, pretty setting in remote attractive village; self-catering cottage
Own brew ~ Licensee Kim Mathews ~ Real ale ~ Bar food (12–2, 6.30–8.30; not Mon or Tues, not Sun evening) ~ Restaurant ~ No credit cards ~ (016974) 78288 ~ Children in eating area of bar and restaurant ~ Dogs welcome ~ Folk 1st Sun of month ~ Open 12–3, 5.30–11; 12–3, 7.30–10.30 Sun; closed Mon and Tues lunchtimes

SANTON BRIDGE
Santon Bridge Inn *Off A595 at Holmrook or Gosforth*
Traditional small Lakeland inn in quiet riverside spot with fell views, turkey carpet, stripped beams, timbered booths, log fire, cheerful service, good drinks range inc big pots of tea, decent bar food, comfortable lounge; picnic-sets outside
Jennings ~ Tenants John Morrow and Lesley Rhodes ~ Real ale ~ Bar food (12–2.30, 6–9.30) ~ Restaurant ~ (01946) 726221 ~ Children welcome ~ Dogs allowed in bar and bedrooms ~ Open 11–11; 12–10.30 Sun ~ Bedrooms: £40(£45B)/£55(£60B)

ULVERSTON
Bay Horse *Canal Foot signposted off A590 and then you wend your way past the huge Glaxo factory*
Smart and civilised small hotel with very good imaginative lunchtime bar food and stylish evening meals, no smoking conservatory restaurant with fine views over Morecambe Bay (as have the comfortable bedrooms) and there are

some seats out on the terrace; please note, the bedroom price includes dinner as well
Free house ~ Licensee Robert Lyons ~ Real ale ~ Bar food (bar food lunchtime only; not Mon) ~ Restaurant ~ (01229) 583972 ~ Children in eating area of bar and in restaurant if over 12 ~ Dogs allowed in bar and bedrooms ~ Open 11–11; 12–10.30 Sun ~ Bedrooms: /£165B

DERBYSHIRE

Dog Friendly Hotels and B&Bs

ASHBOURNE Callow Hall *Mappleton Rd, Ashbourne, Derbyshire DE6 2AA* (01335) 300900 **£130**, plus special breaks; 16 lovely well furnished rms, excellent bthrms. Quietly smart and friendly Victorian mansion up a long drive through grounds with fine trees and surrounded by marvellous countryside; comfortable drawing room with open fire, fresh flowers and plants, and period furniture, very good traditional food using home-grown produce, excellent breakfasts, and kind hosts; good private fishing; cl Christmas; disabled access; dogs welcome in bedrooms
BAKEWELL Hassop Hall *Hassop, Bakewell, Derbyshire DE45 1NS* (01629) 640488 **£98.90**, plus winter breaks; 13 gracious rms. Mentioned in the Domesday Book, in lovely parkland surrounded by fine scenery, this handsome hotel has antiques and oil paintings, an elegant drawing room, oak-panelled bar, good food and friendly service; tennis; no accommodation 3 nights over Christmas; partial disabled access; dogs welcome in bedrooms

BIGGIN-BY-HARTINGTON Biggin Hall *Biggin-by-Hartington, Buxton, Derbyshire SK17 0DH (01298) 84451* **£70**, plus special breaks; 19 spacious rms with antiques, some in converted 18th-c stone building and in bothy. Cheerfully run 17th-c house in quiet grounds with a very relaxed atmosphere, two comfortable sitting rooms, log fires, freshly cooked straightforward food with an emphasis on free-range wholefoods served at 7pm in the attractive dining room, and packed lunches if wanted; children 12 and over; limited disabled access; dogs welcome in bedrooms

BIRCH VALE Waltzing Weasel *New Mills Rd, Birch Vale, High Peak, Derbyshire SK22 1BT (01663) 743402* **£75**; 8 lovely rms. Attractive traditional inn with open fire, some handsome furnishings, daily papers and plants in quiet civilised bar, very good food using the best seasonal produce in charming back restaurant (fine views), excellent puddings and cheeses, obliging service; children over 7 in restaurant; disabled access; dogs welcome

DOVE DALE Peveril of the Peak *Thorpe, Ashbourne, Derbyshire DE6 2AW (08704) 008109* **£89**, plus special breaks; 46 rms. Relaxing hotel in pretty village with comfortable sofas and log fire in lounge, modern bar and attractive restaurant overlooking the garden, and good English cooking; tennis; wonderful walking nearby; disabled access; dogs welcome in bedrooms

GRINDLEFORD Maynard Arms *Main Rd, Nether Padley, Grindleford, Hope Valley, Derbyshire S32 2HE (01433) 630321* **£79***, plus special breaks; 10 rms. Comfortable hotel with log fire and good Peak District views from the first-floor lounge, smart welcoming bar, good choice of food, popular evening restaurant, and particularly attentive service; good walks nearby; dogs welcome in bedrooms

HATHERSAGE George *Main Rd, Hathersage, Hope Valley, Derbyshire S32 1BB (01433) 650436* **£120**, plus special breaks; 19 pretty rms (the back ones are quietest). Substantial and comfortably modernised old inn with attractive airy lounge, beamed friendly bar, popular food, and a neat flagstoned back terrace by rose garden; good walks all around; dogs welcome in bedrooms

HOPE Underleigh House *Edale Rd, Hope, Castleton, Derbyshire S33 6RF (01433) 621372* **£69***, plus special breaks; 6 thoughtfully decorated rms. In unspoilt countryside, this spotlessly kept converted barn has fine views from the comfortable sitting room, hearty breakfasts with good home-made preserves enjoyed around communal table in flagstoned dining room, friendly cheerful owners, attractive gardens; terrific walks on the doorstep, packed lunches can be arranged; cl Christmas and New Year; children over 12; dogs by arrangement

KIRK IRETON Barley Mow *Kirk Ireton, Ashbourne, Derbyshire DE6 3JP (01335) 370306* **£45**; 5 rms. Tall, Jacobean, walkers' inn with lots of woodwork in series of interconnecting bar rooms, a solid fuel stove in beamed residents' sitting room, and well kept real ales; close to Carsington Reservoir; cl Christmas wk; dogs in one ground floor room

MATLOCK Riber Hall *Matlock, Derbyshire DE4 5JU (01629) 582795* **£136**, plus special breaks; 14 lovely beamed rms with antiques, chocolates and baskets of fruit. Elizabethan manor house in pretty grounds surrounded by peaceful countryside, with antiques-filled heavily beamed rooms, fresh flowers, two elegant dining rooms with enjoyable food and fine wines, and tennis and clay pigeon shooting; children over 10; dogs welcome in bedrooms

MONSAL HEAD Monsal Head Hotel *Monsal Head, Buxton, Derbyshire DE45 1NL (01629) 640250* **£50**, plus special breaks; 7 very good rms, some with lovely views. Comfortable and enjoyable small hotel in marvellous setting high above the River Wye, with horsey theme in bar (converted from old stables), freshly prepared decent food using seasonal produce, and good service; cl 25 Dec; dogs welcome in bedrooms

ROWSLEY Peacock *Rowsley, Matlock, Derbyshire DE4 2EB (01629) 733518* **£125**, plus special breaks; 16 comfortable rms. 17th-c country house hotel by River Derwent (private fishing in season), with well kept gardens, friendly staff, interesting old-fashioned inner bar, spacious lounge, and very popular restaurant; dogs welcome in bedrooms

Dog Friendly Pubs

BUXTON
Bull i' th' Thorn *Ashbourne Road (A515) six miles S of Buxton, nr Hurdlow*
Handy for the High Peak Trail, this is a curious cross between a medieval hall with lots of interesting things to look at, and a straightforward roadside pub with the usual food, drinks and so forth – well worth a stop; plenty of tables outside
Robinsons ~ Tenant Peter Atkins ~ Real ale ~ Bar food (12–2.30, 6–9; 12–8 Sun) ~ (01298) 83348 ~ Children welcome ~ Dogs allowed in bar and bedrooms ~ Open 12–3, 6–11; 12–10.30 Sun ~ Bedrooms: 1£60B
FROGGATT EDGE
Chequers *off A623 N of Bakewell; OS Sheet 119, B6054, map reference 247761*

Prettily set country inn with peaceful back garden, and the Edge itself just up through the woods behind; good interesting food in rather smart bar with antique prints, efficient helpful staff

Pubmaster ~ Tenants Jonathan and Joanna Tindall ~ Real ale ~ Bar food (12–2, 6–9.30; 12–9.30 Sat; 12–9 Sun) ~ (01433) 630231 ~ Children welcome ~ Dogs allowed in bedrooms ~ Open 12–3, 5–11; 12–11 Sat; 12–10.30 Sun; closed 25 Dec ~ Bedrooms: /£64B

LADYBOWER RESERVOIR
Yorkshire Bridge *A6013 N of Bamford*

Attractively placed near lots of pleasant countryside walks, nicely bustling atmosphere in several distinctive areas varying from country-cottage through light and airy to valley-view conservatory, enjoyable generous bar food with lots of traditional dishes; comfortable bedrooms, handy for walks above the Ladybower, Derwent and Howden reservoirs

Free house ~ Licensees Trevelyan and John Illingworth ~ Real ale ~ Bar food (12–2, 6–9(9.30 Fri and Sat); 12–8.30 Sun) ~ Restaurant ~ (01433) 651361 ~ Children in eating area of bar and restaurant ~ Dogs welcome ~ Open 11–11; 12–10.30 Sun ~ Bedrooms: £45B/£62B

LITTON
Red Lion *Village signposted off A623, between B6465 and B6049 junctions; also signposted off B6049*

17th-c village pub with blazing fires in homely low-beamed linked front rooms, bigger no smoking back room, good drinks choice, exceptionally friendly staff, enjoyable food inc very good value hot and cold sandwiches; good walks nearby

Free house ~ Licensees Terry and Michele Vernon ~ Real ale ~

Bar food (12–2, 6–8(8.30 Thurs–Sat); not Sun evenings) ~ (01298) 871458 ~ Well behaved children over 6 till 8pm ~ Dogs welcome ~ Open 12–3, 6–11; 12–11 Sat; 12–10.30 Sun

SHARDLOW

Old Crown *3 miles from M1 junction 24, via A50: at first B6540 exit from A50 (just under 2 miles) turn off towards Shardlow – pub E of Shardlow itself, at Cavendish Bridge, actually just over Leics boundary*

Welcoming 17th-c coaching inn, cheerful beamed bar packed with hundreds of jugs and mugs, masses of bric-a-brac, friendly staff, good beers and malt whiskies, popular bar food; cellar restaurant with terrace overlooking garden

Free house ~ Licensees Peter and Gillian Morton-Harrison ~ Real ale ~ Bar food (lunchtime) ~ (01332) 792392 ~ Children in eating area of bar ~ Dogs allowed in bar ~ Open 11.30–3.30, 5–11; 12–4.30, 7–10.30 Sun; closed 25 and 26 Dec ~ Bedrooms: £30S/£40S

DEVON
Exeter & East Devon

Dog Friendly Hotels and B&Bs

EXETER Edwardian Hotel *30–32 Heavitree Rd, Exeter, Devon EX1 2LQ (01392) 276102* **£56**, plus special breaks; 12 individually furnished rms, 4 with four-posters. Popular guest house close to cathedral and city centre, with pretty lounge, enjoyable breakfasts in attractive dining rooms, and warmly friendly and knowledgeable resident owners; plenty of places nearby for evening meals; cl 25–26 Dec; dogs welcome in bedrooms

EXETER Hotel Barcelona *Magdalen Street, Exeter, Devon EX2 4HY (01392) 281000* **£106**; 46 beautifully furnished rms with CD-player and video, and lovely bthrms. Stylishly modern, converted Victorian eye hospital filled with bright posters and paintings, a bar with 1950s-style furniture and fashionable cocktails, a smart but informal no smoking restaurant overlooking the big walled garden, with a wood-burning grill and wood-burning pizza oven plus other good-value contemporary choices, a nightclub showing 1950s films noirs, and very helpful staff; disabled access; dogs welcome in bedrooms

EXETER St Olaves Court *Mary Arches St, Exeter, Devon EX4 3AZ (01392) 217736* **£123**w, plus special breaks; 14 lovely rms. Handsome Georgian-style house just 400 yds from the cathedral in its own walled garden, with a warm welcome from helpful friendly staff, comfortable rooms, enjoyable evening meals in candlelit restaurant, and good breakfasts; dogs welcome away from restaurant

GITTISHAM Combe House *Gittisham, Honiton, Devon EX14 0AD (01404) 540400* **£138**, plus winter breaks; 15 individually decorated pretty rms with lovely views. Peaceful Elizabethan country hotel in gardens with 700-year-old cedar of Lebanon, and walks around the 3,000-acre estate; elegant day rooms with antiques, pictures and fresh flowers, a happy relaxed atmosphere, very good food using some home-grown produce, and fine wines (the cellar is popular for wine tastings); can use the house for special occasions and meetings; dogs welcome in bedrooms

MEMBURY Lea Hill *Membury, Axminster, Devon EX13 7AQ (01404) 881881* **£70**; 4 individually furnished rms. Thatched, no smoking 14th-c longhouse in 8 acres of secluded grounds inc their own par 3, 9-hole golf course, and lovely views; comfortable beamed rooms with inglenook fireplaces, a convivial bar, relaxed and friendly owners, and nice breakfasts, morning coffee, and afternoon tea; self-catering, too; no children; dogs welcome in bedrooms

STOCKLAND Kings Arms *Stockland, Honiton, Devon EX14 9BS (01404) 881361* **£50**; 3 rms. Cream-faced thatched pub with elegant rooms, open fires, first-class food in bar and evening restaurant food (esp fish), and interesting wine list; skittle alley, live music Sat, Sun pm; cl 25 Dec; dogs welcome

NORTH DEVON & EXMOOR

Dog Friendly Hotels and B&Bs

BISHOP'S TAWTON Halmpstone Manor *Bishops Tawton, Barnstaple, Devon EX32 0EA (01271) 830321* **£100**; 5 pretty rms. Quietly relaxing small country hotel with log fire in comfortable sitting room, enjoyable food in panelled dining room, good breakfasts, caring service, an attractive garden, and nice views; plenty to do nearby; cl Christmas, New Year, and Feb; dogs welcome

BUCKLAND BREWER Coach & Horses *Buckland Brewer, Bideford, Devon EX39 5LU (01237) 451395* **£60**; 2 rms above bar (so could be noisy for children until 11.30pm). Welcoming well preserved 13th-c thatched village pub with cosy beamed bar, log fires in inglenook fireplaces, enjoyable food, dining room, and pleasant garden; partial disabled access; dogs in bar on lead

CLAWTON Court Barn Hotel *Clawton, Holsworthy, Devon EX22 6PS (01409) 271219* **£66**, plus special breaks; 8 individually furnished rms. Charming, recently refurbished country house in five pretty acres with croquet, 9-hole putting green, small chip-and-putt course, and tennis and badminton courts; comfortable lounges, log fires, library/TV room, good service, imaginative food and award-winning wines (and teas), and a quiet relaxed atmosphere; they are kind to families; cl first 2 wks Jan; dogs welcome in bedrooms

HEDDON'S MOUTH Heddon's Gate Hotel *Martinhoe, Parracombe, Barnstaple, Devon EX31 4PZ (01598) 763313* **£138.80** inc dinner, plus special breaks; 14 comfortable rms named for their original use and many with views. Victorian country house hotel in interesting large gardens on the edge of Exmoor, with marvellously relaxed and friendly atmosphere, comfortable sitting room with lovely views, good library/Victorian morning room, attractive dining room, very good home cooking inc 6-course dinners and proper afternoon tea, and friendly helpful service; cl Nov–Easter; children welcome if able to eat at 8pm (no special meals for them); disabled access in annexe cottage; dogs welcome away from dining room

LYNMOUTH Rising Sun *Mars Hill, Lynmouth, Devon EX35 6EG (01598) 753223* **£99**, plus special breaks; 16 comfortable and cosy rms. Thatched 14th-c inn with lovely views over the little harbour and out to sea, oak-panelled dining room, beamed and panelled bar with uneven oak floors, good food and wines, charming terraced garden, and lots of nearby walks; children over 7; dogs welcome in bedrooms

NORTHAM Yeoldon House *Durrant Lane, Northam, Bideford, Devon EX39 2RL (01237) 474400* **£90**, plus special breaks; 10 individually decorated rms. Quietly set hotel in two acres by the River Torridge, with a warmly friendly and relaxed atmosphere, a comfortable lounge, good food using local produce in the attractive dining room, and helpful service; lots to do nearby; cl Christmas; dogs welcome away from restaurant

PORLOCK Oaks *Doverhay, Porlock, Minehead, Somerset TA24 8ES (01643) 862265* **£100***, plus special breaks; 9 airy and pretty rms. Particularly welcoming and spotless Edwardian country house looking down from Exmoor to Porlock Bay, with surrounding lawns and oak trees, a relaxed atmosphere and log fire in attractive lounge, and good unpretentious cooking in attractive no smoking restaurant; cl Nov–Mar; children over 8; dogs welcome in bedrooms

PORLOCK Seapoint *Redway, Porlock, Minehead, Somerset TA24 8QE (01643) 862289* **£52***, plus winter breaks; 3 rms. Surrounded by the Exmoor hills and with views of Porlock Bay, this no smoking Edwardian guesthouse has a comfortable sitting room with winter log fire, a friendly and relaxing atmosphere, enjoyable home-made food in candlelit dining room, and fine breakfasts; cl Dec–Jan; they are kind to children; dogs welcome away from dining area

SELWORTHY Hindon Farm *Selworthy, Minehead, Somerset TA24 8SH (01643) 705244* **£48***; 2 rms. Organic Exmoor farm of 500 acres with sheep, pigs, cattle, donkeys and ducks, lots of lovely surrounding walks inc award-winning conservation trail, riding (can bring your own horse), and mountain biking; games barn with table tennis and snooker, log fires, and fine breakfasts using their own eggs, bacon, honey, and bread; self-catering farmhouse wing plus cottage, and organic produce basket on arrival; organic farm shop also; children under 11 by arrangement in B&B; dogs welcome in bedrooms

SHEEPWASH Half Moon *Sheepwash, Beaworthy, Devon EX21 5NE (01409) 231376* **£80**, plus special breaks; 14 rms inc 5 newly refurbished ones in stables. Civilised heart-of-Devon hideaway in colourful village square with 10 miles of private salmon, sea trout and brown trout fishing on the Torridge, a neatly kept friendly bar, solid old furnishings and big log fire, good wines, lovely evening restaurant, lunchtime bar snacks; cl 20–27 Dec; limited disabled access; dogs welcome away from dining room

South Devon & Dartmoor

Dog Friendly Hotels and B&Bs

ASHBURTON Holne Chase *Ashburton, Newton Abbot, Devon TQ13 7NS (01364) 631471* **£150**, plus winter breaks; 17 comfortable and individually furnished rms, many with views over the Dart Valley, and some split-level suites in converted stables. Marvellously peaceful ex-hunting lodge of Buckfast Abbey in 70 acres with sweeping lawns and plenty of woodland walks, a mile of Dart fishing, shooting and riding on Dartmoor; cheerful welcoming owners, comfortable public rooms with log fires, very good modern English cooking using home-grown vegetables, and enjoyable breakfasts and afternoon teas (home-made breads, marmalades and so forth); children over 12 in evening restaurant; dogs welcome

BLACKAWTON Normandy Arms *Blackawton, Totnes, Devon TQ9 7BN (01803) 712316* **£58***, plus special breaks; 4 pretty rms. Quaint friendly pub in quiet village, with cosy main bar, log fire, some interesting displays of World War II battle gear, generous food in bar and restaurant, real ales, and seats in garden; dogs welcome

BOVEY TRACEY Edgemoor Hotel *Haytor Rd, Bovey Tracey, Newton Abbot, Devon TQ13 9LE (01626) 832466* **£99.50***, plus special breaks; 16 charming rms. Ivy-covered country house in neatly kept gardens on the edge of Dartmoor, with comfortable lounge and bar, log fires, good food in elegant restaurant; cl 1 wk after Christmas; children over 10; limited disabled access; dogs welcome away from food areas

CHAGFORD Easton Court *Sandy Park, Chagford, Newton Abbot, Devon TQ13 8JN (01647) 433469* **£140** inc dinner, plus special breaks; 8 redecorated rms. Creeper-clad, thatched and newly refurbished 15th-c house with beams, inglenook fireplace, granite walls, and big library (literary connections inc Evelyn Waugh writing *Brideshead Revisited* here), cosy bar, charming sitting room, good breakfasts, delicious evening meals in candlelit restaurant; cl Jan; children over 12; dogs welcome in bedrooms

CHAGFORD Gidleigh Park *Chagford, Newton Abbot, Devon TQ13 8HH (01647) 432367* **£410** inc dinner, plus winter breaks; 15 opulent and individual rms with fruit and flowers. Exceptional luxurious Dartmoor-edge mock-Tudor hotel with deeply comfortable panelled drawing room, wonderful flowers, conservatory overlooking the fine grounds (40 acres, with walks straight up on to the moor), log fires, particularly fine cooking and a fine wine list, and caring staff; children over 7 in restaurant; dogs welcome in bedrooms

DARTMOUTH Ford House *44 Victoria Rd, Dartmouth, Devon TQ6 9DX (01803) 834047* **£85**, plus special breaks; 4 individually decorated rms. Nr the harbour, this Regency town house has a log fire in the comfortable drawing room, antiques, good interesting food using fresh local produce eaten around a big table, delicious breakfasts, helpful service, and sheltered garden; you can take over the whole house for a wknd party; cl Nov–Mar; dogs welcome

DARTMOUTH Gunfield Hotel *Castle Road, Dartmouth, Devon TQ6 0JN (01803) 834571* **£95**; 10 rms with views of the river. In waterside gardens overlooking the estuary, this informal and friendly hotel has a convivial bar, cheerful staff, an attractive airy dining room serving enjoyable food, and an outside decked eating area overlooking the water; water taxi into Dartmouth, and their own motor-boats; dogs in bedrooms and on lead in bar

DARTMOUTH Royal Castle *11 The Quay, Dartmouth, Devon TQ6 9PS (01803) 833033* **£119.90**, plus special breaks; 25 individually furnished rms. Well restored mainly Georgian hotel (part 16th c) overlooking the inner harbour – great views from most rooms; lively and interesting public bar with open fires and beams, quiet library/lounge with antiques, drawing room overlooking the quayside, winter spit-roasts in lounge bar, elegant upstairs seafood restaurant, decent bar food, and friendly staff; dogs welcome in bedrooms

DODDISCOMBSLEIGH Nobody Inn *Doddiscombsleigh, Exeter, Devon EX6 7PS (01647) 252394* **£70***; 7 rms, some in a Georgian manor house 150 yds down the road, and most with own bthrm. Friendly 16th-c pub with beams, heavy wooden furniture, and inglenook fireplace in the attractively furnished two-roomed lounge bar, an outstanding cellar running to 800 (fairly priced) wines and 250 malts, and popular food in bar and restaurant inc huge range of Devon cheeses; good views from garden, and the church is worth visiting for fine stained glass; cl 25–26 Dec; no children; dogs welcome

DREWSTEIGNTON Silkhouse *Drewsteignton, Exeter, Devon EX6 6RF (01647) 231267* **£60**; 2 rms. Quietly set, rambling 16th-c longhouse named by the Huguenots who wove silk here; low beams, fine paintings, antiques and r ichly coloured fabrics and paintwork, a relaxed atmosphere, imaginative food in low-ceilinged dining room; and a really lovely garden with ponds and streams, lots of wildlife, and all-weather tennis court; horses welcome; no children; dogs welcome

HAYTOR Bel Alp House *Haytor, Newton Abbot, Devon TQ13 9XX (01364) 661217* **£120***, plus special breaks; 8 spacious rms. Handsome Edwardian country house with elegant drawing room, comfortable sitting room, log fires and lots of fresh flowers and plants, friendly atmosphere, and fine careful cooking in pretty restaurant; wonderful views and peaceful garden; cl 21 Dec–12 Jan; disabled access; dogs welcome in bedrooms

HAYTOR VALE Rock *Haytor Vale, Newton Abbot, Devon TQ13 9XP (01364) 661305* **£85.50***, plus special breaks; 9 individual rms. Civilised old coaching inn on the edge of Dartmoor National Park, with good food (inc fresh fish), a nice mix of visitors and locals in the two rooms of the panelled bar, open fires, no smoking restaurant, courteous service, and big garden; walking, fishing, riding and golf nearby; cl 25 Dec; dogs welcome in bedrooms

HEXWORTHY Forest Inn *Hexworthy, Princetown, Yelverton, Devon PL20 6SD (01364) 631211* **£59**; 10 cosy, comfortable rms. Country inn in fine Dartmoor setting, popular with walkers and anglers; varied menu in both bar and restaurant, local ales, good choice of wines, and welcoming staff; cl Jan; dogs welcome

HOLNE Wellpritton Farm *Holne, Ashburton, Devon TQ13 7RX (01364) 631273* **£45***, plus special breaks; 5 pretty rms. Small, recently refurbished friendly Dartmoor farm set in 15 acres with horses, goats and chickens and lovely views from terrace and garden; comfortable sitting room, good, completely home-made evening meals using local produce, and enjoyable breakfasts; children under 5 by arrangement; dogs welcome in bedrooms

LEWDOWN Lewtrenchard Manor *Lewdown, Okehampton, Devon EX20 4PN (01566) 783256* **£175**, plus special breaks; 9 well equipped rms with fresh flowers and period furniture. Lovely Elizabethan manor house in garden with fine dovecot and surrounded by peaceful estate with shooting, fishing and croquet; dark panelling, ornate ceilings, antiques, fresh flowers, and log fires, a friendly welcome, relaxed atmosphere, and candlelit restaurant with very good imaginative food; children over 8; partial disabled access; dogs welcome in bedrooms

LIFTON Arundell Arms *Fore St, Lifton, Devon PL16 0AA (01566) 784666* **£120**, plus special breaks; 28 well equipped rms, 5 in annexe over the road. Carefully renovated old coaching inn with 20 miles of its own waters – salmon and trout fishing and a long-established fly-fishing school; comfortable sitting room, log fires, super food in both bar and elegant restaurant, carefully chosen wines, and kind service from local staff; new eating area in attractive terraced garden; cl 4 days over Christmas; dogs allowed away from restaurant and river bank

MALBOROUGH Soar Mill Cove Hotel *Malborough, Salcombe, Devon TQ7 3DS (01548) 561566* **£218**, plus special breaks; 21 comfortable rms, some opening on to garden. Neatly kept single-storey building in idyllic spot by peaceful and very beautiful cove on NT coast (excellent walks), with lovely views, extensive private grounds, tennis/putting, and warm indoor pool; outstanding service, log fires, very good food (marvellous fish), and they are particularly kind to children of all ages: microwave, fridge, and so forth for little ones, own high tea or smaller helpings of most meals, fully equipped laundry, a play room, table tennis and snooker, swings, and donkey and pony; by Feb, a new restaurant, lounge and coffee shop will have opened; cl Jan; disabled access; dogs welcome in bedrooms

MORETONHAMPSTEAD Great Sloncombe Farm *Moretonhampstead, Newton Abbot, Devon TQ13 8QF (01647) 440595* **£48***; 3 rms – the big double is the favourite. Lovely 13th-c farmhouse on a working dairy and stock farm, with friendly owners, carefully polished old-fashioned furniture in oak-beamed lounge, decent food, hearty breakfasts, log fires, a relaxed atmosphere, and good nearby walking and bird-watching; no smoking; children over 8; dogs welcome in bedrooms

NORTH BOVEY Gate House *North Bovey, Newton Abbot, Devon TQ13 8RB (01647) 440479* **£60***, plus special breaks; 3 charming rms. 15th-c thatched cottage in picturesque village, with huge granite fireplace in attractive beamed sitting room, breakfasts and candlelit evening meals in beamed dining room, tea with home-made cakes, friendly owners, and outdoor swimming pool in peaceful garden; plenty to do nearby; no children; dogs welcome in bedrooms

SALCOMBE Tides Reach *Cliff Rd, South Sands, Salcombe, Devon TQ8 8LJ (01548) 843466* **£142**, plus special breaks; 35 rms, many with estuary views. Unusually individual resort hotel run by long-serving owners in pretty wooded cove by the sea, with airy luxury day rooms, big sea aquarium in cocktail bar, good restaurant food using fresh local produce, friendly efficient service, and squash, snooker, leisure complex, health area, and big heated pool; windsurfing etc, beach over lane, and lots of coast walks; cl Dec–Jan; children over 8; dogs welcome in bedrooms

SANDY PARK Mill End *Sandy Park, Chagford, Newton Abbot, Devon TQ13 8JN (01647) 432282* **£120***, plus special breaks; 15 attractive rms with fine bthrms and views. Quietly set former flour mill with waterwheel in neatly kept grounds below Dartmoor with 600 yards of private salmon and trout fishing, access to miles of game fishing and still water fishing on local lakes; comfortably refurbished lounges, carefully prepared interesting food, fine breakfasts, and cream teas on the lawn, and good service; cl Jan; partial disabled access; dogs welcome in bedrooms

SOUTH ZEAL Oxenham Arms *South Zeal, Okehampton, Devon EX20 2JT (01837) 840244* **£60**, plus special breaks; 8 rms. Grandly atmospheric old inn dating back to 12th c and first licensed in 1477 (a neolithic standing stone still forms part of the wall in the TV room); elegant beamed and pan-elled bar with chatty relaxed atmosphere and open fire, a wide choice of enjoyable food and wines, and charming ex-monastery small garden; dogs welcome away from dining room

STAVERTON Sea Trout *Staverton, Totnes, Devon TQ9 6PA (01803) 762274* **£74**; 10 cottagey rms. Comfortable pub in quiet hamlet nr River Dart with two relaxed beamed bars, log fires, popular food in bar and airy dining conservatory, and terraced garden with fountains and waterfalls; cl Christmas; disabled access; dogs welcome away from restaurant

STOKE GABRIEL Gabriel Court *Stoke Gabriel, Totnes, Devon TQ9 6SF (01803) 782206* **£84**, plus special breaks; 19 rms, some in former hay lofts. In a walled Elizabethan garden, this attractive family-run manor has quiet relaxing lounges (winter log fire), enjoyable traditional English food, and courteous helpful staff; outdoor heated swimming pool and croquet lawn; dogs welcome away from dining room

TWO BRIDGES Prince Hall *Two Bridges, Yelverton, Devon PL20 6SA (01822) 890403* **£105**, plus special breaks; 8 attractive spacious rms. Surrounded by Dartmoor National Park, this tranquil, recently refurbished 18th-c country house is run by caring friendly owners and their helpful staff; lovely views from convivial bar, comfortable sitting room, and cosy dining room, open fires, very good evening meals, enjoyable breakfasts, and lots of fine walks; cl mid-Dec to mid-Feb; children over 10; dogs welcome

Dog Friendly Pubs

BEER
Dolphin *Fore Street, off B3174 W of Seaton*
Just up the steep lane from the beach, friendly and bustling seaside local with old-fashioned décor and all sorts of interesting nooks and bric-a-brac; well kept ales, enjoyable food inc good local fish, one or two tables out by the pavement
Free house ~ Licensee Mrs Lee Gibbs ~ Real ale ~ Bar food ~ Restaurant ~ No credit cards ~ (01297) 20068 ~ Children welcome ~ Dogs welcome ~ Open 11–3, 6–11; 12–3, 6.30–11 Sun ~ Bedrooms: £26S/£42(£52B)

BRANSCOMBE

Fountain Head *Upper village, above the robust old church; village signposted off A3052 Sidmouth–Seaton, then from Branscombe Square follow road up hill towards Sidmouth, and after about a mile turn left after the church; OS Sheet 192, map reference 188889*

Friendly and old-fashioned, with a lot of character (the main high-beamed bar still has the raised fireplace of its days as a forge), its own good small brewery, popular bar food, and seats out by a little stream; the Airedale is called Max, and they offer self-catering

Own brew ~ Licensee Mrs Catherine Luxton ~ Real ale ~ Bar food (not 25 Dec) ~ (01297) 680359 ~ Children in own room; must be over 10 in evening restaurant ~ Dogs welcome ~ Folk/Irish summer Thurs ~ Open 11.30–3, 6–11; 12–3, 6–10.30 Sun; 11.30–2.30, 6.30–11 in winter

CHAGFORD

Ring o' Bells *Off A382 Moretonhampstead–Whiddon Down*

Quietly civilised oak-panelled bar with dog biscuits on the corner of the counter (though pub cat Coriander keeps visiting dogs in order), small no smoking candlelit dining room, good generous food using local game, meat and fresh fish; seats in sunny walled garden behind, nearby moorland walks

Free house ~ Licensee Mrs Judith Pool ~ Real ale ~ Bar food (they serve breakfast and snacks from 8.30am) ~ (01647) 432466 ~ Children over 10 in eating area of bar; younger children in restaurant but no pushchairs ~ Dogs welcome ~ Open 11–3, 5–11; 12–3, 6–10.30 Sun; may close early on quiet evenings in winter ~ Bedrooms: £20/£40(£45S)

DOLTON

Union *B3217*

Two-bar village inn with beams, country bric-a-brac, some

antique furnishings, chatty atmosphere, tasty bar food using local produce, some rustic tables outside; comfortable bedrooms

Free house ~ Licensees Ian and Irene Fisher ~ Real ale ~ Bar food (not Weds) ~ Restaurant ~ (01805) 804633 ~ Children in eating area of bar (until 9) and in restaurant ~ Dogs allowed in bar and bedrooms ~ Open 12–2.30, 6–11; 12–2.30, 7–10.30 Sun; closed Weds and 1st 2 wks Feb ~ Bedrooms: /£55S(£65B)

EXMINSTER

Turf Hotel *Follow the signs to the Swan's Nest, signposted from A739 S of village, then continue to end of track, by gates; park, and walk right along canal towpath – nearly a mile; there's a fine seaview out to the mudflats at low tide*

Fine isolated coastal pub with pews and woodburner in airy bare-boards bar, bay window views of tidal flats, good bar food inc popular cook-your-own-barbecue menu (not winter), good drinks choice, garden with play area built around former lifeboat; they run boats here from Countess Wear or Topsham quay

Free house ~ Licensees Clive and Ginny Redfern ~ Real ale ~ Bar food (12–2.30(3 Sat and Sun), 7–9) ~ (01392) 833128 ~ Children welcome ~ Dogs welcome ~ Open 11.30–11; 11.30–10.30 Sun; closed Nov–Feb ~ Bedrooms: £30/£60

HOLBETON

Mildmay Colours *Signposted off A379 W of A3121 junction*

Neat and friendly bar with horse racing memorabilia and some stripped stone, good beers and local farm cider, decent straightforward bar food, well kept garden has picnic-sets, a swing, and an aviary

Free house ~ Licensee Louise Price ~ Real ale ~ Bar food ~ Restaurant ~ (01752) 830248 ~ Children in family room ~ Dogs welcome ~ Open 11–3, 6–11; 12–3, 7–10.30 Sun ~ Bedrooms: £32.50B/£50B

HORNDON

Elephants Nest *If coming from Okehampton on A386 turn left at Mary Tavy Inn, then left after about ½ mile; pub signposted beside Mary Tavy Inn, then Horndon signposted; on the Ordnance Survey Outdoor Leisure Map it's named as the New Inn*

Good log fire, flagstones, beams and boards for this distinctive 16th-c pub; decent home-made bar food, well kept beers, quite a few pub pets; benches on the spacious lawn look over the pastures of Dartmoor's lower slopes, and the rougher moorland above

Free house ~ Licensee Peter Wolfes ~ Real ale ~ Bar food (11.30–2, 6.30–10(9.30 Sun)) ~ Restaurant ~ (01822) 810273 ~ Children in family room ~ Dogs welcome ~ Open 11.30(12 Sun)–2.30, 6.30–11(10.30 Sun)

LUSTLEIGH

Cleave *Village signposted off A382 Bovey Tracey–Moretonhampstead*

Lovely old thatched pub with antique settles and roaring log fire in low-ceilinged granite bar, decent food, well equipped family room, wendy house in flower-filled sheltered garden

Heavitree ~ Tenant A Perring ~ Real ale ~ Bar food (all day Sat and Sun in summer) ~ Restaurant ~ (01647) 277223 ~ Children in family room and in restaurant if over 8 ~ Dogs welcome ~ Open 11.30–3, 6–11; 11–11 Sat; 12–10.30 Sun; closed Mon Nov–Feb

LYDFORD

Castle Inn *Village signposted off A386 Okehampton–Tavistock*

Interestingly furnished old-fashioned two-room heavy-beamed bar in pub by ruined 12th-c castle and close to a beautiful river gorge (which is owned by the National Trust; cl Nov–Easter)

Heavitree ~ Manager Terence Jackson ~ Real ale ~ Bar food ~
Restaurant ~ (01822) 820241 ~ Children in eating area of bar
and in restaurant ~ Dogs welcome ~ Open 11–11; 12–11 Sun
~ Bedrooms: £70B/£95B

MOLLAND

London *Village signposted off B3227 E of South Molton, down
narrow lanes*

Real old Exmoor, with a water-bowl by the good log fire for the
working-dog regulars, strong sporting links, proper farm cider
as well as good beers tapped from casks, and an easy chatty mix
in the highly traditional bar and panelled dining room with its
great curved settle; good value home cooking, a cheerful
welcome, country views from a few picnic-sets out in front
*Free house ~ Licensees M J and L J Short ~ Real ale ~ Bar food
~ Restaurant ~ No credit cards ~ (01769) 550269 ~ Children
in family room ~ Dogs welcome ~ Open 11.30–2.30, 6–11;
12–2.30, 7–10.30 Sun ~ Bedrooms: /£46B*

NOSS MAYO

Ship *Off A379 via B3186, E of Plymouth*

Friendly and chatty 16th-c pub on tidal inlet, log fires, books
and local pictures, good inventive food strong on local
produce, good drinks choice, helpful staff; tables outside
*Free house ~ Licensees Lesley and Bruce Brunning ~ Real ale ~
Bar food (12–9.30) ~ Restaurant ~ (01752) 872387 ~ Children
in eating area of bar until 7.30 ~ Dogs allowed in bar ~ Open
11.30–11; 12–10.30 Sun*

PETER TAVY

Peter Tavy Inn *Off A386 nr Mary Tavy, N of Tavistock*

Attractive old stone inn, low-beamed bar with high-backed
settles on flagstones by big log fire, good very popular food,
friendly efficient service, good drinks choice; picnic-sets in
pretty garden with peaceful views of Dartmoor rising above
nearby pastures

Free house ~ Licensees Graeme and Karen Sim ~ Real ale ~ Bar food (not 25 Dec) ~ Restaurant ~ (01822) 810348 ~ Children in restaurant ~ Dogs welcome ~ Open 12–2.30(3 Sat), 6.30(6 Sat)–11; 12–3, 6–10.30 Sun; closed 25 Dec

POSTBRIDGE

Warren House *B3212 1½ miles NE of Postbridge*

Great Dartmoor refuge, cosy and unpretentious, with ever-burning fire, easy chairs, settles, beams and partly panelled stripped stone, wild animal pictures, dim lighting, good no-nonsense home cooking and good drinks choice

Free house ~ Licensee Peter Parsons ~ Real ale ~ Bar food (all day summer) ~ Restaurant ~ (01822) 880208 ~ Children in family room ~ Dogs welcome ~ Open 11–11; 12–10.30 Sun; 11–3, 6–11 Mon–Thurs in winter

TOPSHAM

Passage House *Ferry Road, off main street*

Attractive waterside pub with cosy black-beamed traditional bar, lower slate-floored dining area, good fresh fish dishes and straightforward bar food, good drinks; tables out on quiet shoreside terrace

Heavitree ~ Manager Richard Davies ~ Real ale ~ Bar food ~ Restaurant ~ (01392) 873653 ~ Children in restaurant ~ Dogs allowed in bar ~ Open 11–11; 12–10.30 Sun; 11–3, 5–11 weekdays in winter

TUCKENHAY

Maltsters Arms *Take Ashprington road out of Totnes (signed left off A381 on outskirts), keeping on past Watermans Arms*

In a lovely spot with tables out by a peaceful wooded creek, two attractive rooms linked by long narrow bar, a smashing range of drinks, good unusual food, open fires, comfortable bedrooms (there may be a minimum stay of two nights at wknds)

Free house ~ Licensees Denise and Quentin Thwaites ~ Real ale ~ Bar food (12–3, 7–9.30) ~ Restaurant ~ (01803) 732350 ~ Children in eating area of bar and restaurant ~ Dogs allowed in bar ~ Jazz 1st and 3rd Fri of month; outside music in summer ~ Open 11–11; 12–10.30 Sun; closed evening 25 Dec ~ Bedrooms: /£85S

WIDECOMBE

Rugglestone Village at end of B3387; pub just S – turn left at church and NT church house, OS Sheet 191, map reference 720765

Unspoilt local just outside the bustling tourist village, tiny bar with beers and farm cider tapped from the cask, stripped pine in slightly bigger side room, open fires, good simple bar food, friendly service; the cat is called Elbi, the two terriers, Tinker and Belle, and the retriever, Spring; out across the little moorland stream is a field with lots of picnic-sets – no children in the pub, but a big furnished shelter outside

Free house ~ Licensees Lorrie and Moira Ensor ~ Real ale ~ Bar food ~ (01364) 621327 ~ Dogs welcome ~ Open 11–2.30(3 Sat), 6–11; 12–3, 6–10.30 Sun; evening opening 7 in winter

DORSET

Dog Friendly Hotels and B&Bs

BOURNEMOUTH Langtry Manor *26 Derby Rd, Eastcliff, Bournemouth, Dorset BH1 3QB (01202) 553887* **£109.50**, plus special breaks; 27 pretty rms, some in the manor, some in the lodge. Built by Edward VII for Lillie

Langtry, with lots of memorabilia, relaxed public rooms, helpful friendly staff, and good food inc Edwardian dinner every Sat evening; cl 1st 2 wks Jan; no children; disabled access; dogs welcome in bedrooms

BRIDPORT Britmead House *West Bay Rd, Bridport, Dorset DT6 4EG (01308) 422941* **£64**, plus special breaks; 7 rms. Extended Victorian hotel with lots to do nearby, comfortable lounge overlooking garden, attractive dining room, good food, and kind helpful service; disabled access; dogs welcome in bedrooms

DORCHESTER Maiden Castle Farm *Dorchester, Dorset DT2 9PR (01305) 262356* **£52***; 4 rms. Victorian farmhouse in 2 acres of gardens in the heart of Hardy country and set beneath the prehistoric earthworks from which the farm takes its name; views of the hill fort and countryside, and comfortable traditionally furnished sitting room which overlooks the garden; disabled access; dogs welcome in bedrooms

EAST KNIGHTON Countryman *East Knighton, Dorchester, Dorset DT2 8LL (01305) 852666* **£70***; 6 rms. Attractively converted and much liked pair of old cottages with open fires and plenty of character in the main bar which opens into several smaller areas, no smoking family room, half a dozen real ales, imaginative, generously served food inc nice breakfasts and a hot carvery in large restaurant, and courteous staff; cl 25 Dec; dogs welcome

EVERSHOT Summer Lodge *Evershot, Dorchester, Dorset DT2 0JR (01935) 83424* **£205**, plus special breaks; 18 big, individually decorated rms. Beautifully kept, peacefully set former dower house with lovely flowers in the comfortable and elegantly furnished day rooms, excellent food using the best local produce in most attractive restaurant overlooking pretty garden, delicious breakfasts and afternoon tea, and personal caring service; outdoor swimming pool, tennis and croquet; children over 7 in evening restaurant; partial disabled access; dogs welcome in bedrooms

KINGSTON Kingston Country Courtyard *West Street, Kingston, Corfe Castle, Wareham, Dorset BH20 5LH (01929) 481066* **£52***; 10 rms in most attractive farm building conversions. A collection of stylish suites and apartments in beautifully decorated houses keeping much original character and charm, and with wonderful views over Corfe Castle, Arne Peninsula, and the Isle of Wight; enjoyable full English or continental breakfasts in Old Cart Shed dining room; self-catering too; lots to do nearby; cl Dec–Jan; good disabled access; dogs welcome in bedrooms

LOWER BOCKHAMPTON Yalbury Cottage *Lower Bockhampton, Dorchester, Dorset DT2 8PZ (01305) 262382* **£90**, plus special breaks; 8 rms overlooking garden or fields. Very attractive family-run 16th-c thatched house with a relaxed friendly atmosphere, and low beams and inglenook fireplaces in comfortable lounge and dining room; carefully cooked often imaginative food, good wines; cl Jan; dogs welcome in bedrooms

STUDLAND Knoll House *Studland, Swanage, Dorset BH19 3AH (01929) 450450* **£240**; inc lunch and dinner; 80 comfortable rms. Spacious, very well run hotel owned by the same family for over 40 years, in 100 acres with marvellous views of Studland Bay and direct access to the fine 3-mile beach; relaxed friendly atmosphere, particularly helpful staff, super food in dining room with windows overlooking the gardens, cocktail bar, TV lounge, and excellent facilities for families: attractive children's dining room (with proper food and baby food, microwave, own fridge, etc), well equipped play room, table tennis, pool and table football, heated outdoor pool, tennis courts, small private golf course, marvellous adventure playground, and nearby sea fishing, riding, walking, sailing and windsurfing; health spa; cl end Oct–Easter; children over 8 in evening dining room; disabled access; dogs welcome

STURMINSTER NEWTON Plumber Manor *Hazelbury Bryan Road, Plumber, Sturminster Newton, Dorset DT10 2AF (01258) 472507* **£155**, plus special breaks; 16 very comfortable rms, some in nearby period buildings; many in the house itself overlook the peaceful, pretty garden and down the stream with herons and even maybe egrets. Handsome 17th-c, family-run house in quiet countryside, with warm fires, a convivial well stocked bar, attractive writing room/lounge, resident black Labradors, good interesting food inc tempting puddings in three dining rooms, nice breakfasts, a relaxed atmosphere, and exceptionally friendly helpful service; tennis; cl Feb; children welcome by prior arrangement; disabled access; dogs welcome in bedrooms

SYDLING ST NICHOLAS Lamperts Cottage *Sydling St Nicholas, Dorchester, Dorset DT2 9NU (01300) 341659* **£44**; 3 little rms under the eaves, shared bthrms. Charming mainly no smoking 16th-c thatched cottage in unspoilt village, with friendly welcome from helpful owner, good breakfasts in beamed dining room with huge inglenook fireplace and bread oven, and pretty garden; children over 8; dogs welcome in bedrooms

WIMBORNE MINSTER Beechleas *17 Poole Rd, Wimborne, Dorset BH21 1QA (01202) 841684* **£79**, plus special breaks; 9 attractive, comfortable rms. Carefully restored Georgian house with open fires in cosy sitting room and charming dining room, airy conservatory overlooking walled garden, enjoyable Aga-cooked food using organic produce, nice breakfasts, and friendly helpful owners; lots to do and see nearby; cl 24 Dec–mid-Jan; disabled access; dogs welcome in bedrooms

Dog Friendly Pubs

CHIDEOCK
Anchor *Seatown signposted off A35 from Chideock*
Nestling dramatically beneath the 188-metre (617-ft) Golden Cap pinnacle and Dorset Coast path, this well liked pub is just a few steps from the cove beach. Seats and tables on the spacious front terrace are ideally placed for the lovely sea and cliff views; recently refurbished cosy little bars, warming winter fires, friendly cats, sweet-natured black Labrador, decent food, nice simple bedrooms sharing bathroom – you make own breakfast
Palmers ~ Tenants David and Sadie Miles ~ Real ale ~ Bar food (12–9.30 Whitsun–early Sept, not Sun evening Nov–Feb) ~ (01297) 489215 ~ Well behaved children welcome ~ Dogs allowed in bar ~ Jazz, folk and blues Sat evening, some summer Weds evenings ~ Open 11–11; 12–10.30 Sun; 11–2.30, 6–11 winter; closed 25 Dec evening ~ Bedrooms: £25/£50

CHRISTCHURCH
Fishermans Haunt *Winton: B3347 Ringwood road nearly 3 miles N of Christchurch*
Big well run hotel above River Avon and not far from New Forest, several comfortable areas in neat bar, reasonably priced straightforward bar food, tables in attractively planted quiet back garden; a pleasant place to stay
Gales ~ Manager Kevin A Crowley ~ Real ale ~ Bar food ~ Restaurant ~ (01202) 477283 ~ Children welcome ~ Dogs allowed in bar and bedrooms ~ Open 10.30–2.30, 5–11; 10–11

Sat; 12–10.30 Sun ~ Bedrooms: £49.50B/£66B

FARNHAM

Museum Hotel *Village signposted off A354 Blandford Forum–Salisbury*

17th-c thatched inn with cheerfully updated civilised beamed and flagstoned bar, big inglenook fireplace, other distinctive rooms, one with dozens of antlers, excellent drinks choice, very good interesting bar food using local and organic produce; nice bedrooms

Free house ~ Licensees Vicky Elliot and Mark Stephenson ~ Real ale ~ Bar food (till 3 Sun) ~ Restaurant (Fri and Sat evening and Sun lunch) ~ (01725) 516261 ~ Well behaved children over 8 in eating area of bar ~ Dogs allowed in bar and bedrooms ~ Open 12–3, 6–11(7–10.30 Sun); closed 25 Dec, and evenings 26 Dec and 1 Jan ~ Bedrooms: £55B/£85B

PUNCKNOWLE

Crown *Church Street; village signposted off B3157 Bridport–Abbotsbury; or reached off A35 via Chilcombe*

16th-c thatched and heavily beamed two-bar pub opposite partly Norman church, welcoming log fires in big stone fireplaces, cheerful service, reasonably priced generous food, nice view from partly paved back garden

Palmers ~ Tenant Michael Lawless ~ Real ale ~ Bar food (not 25 Dec) ~ No credit cards ~ (01308) 897711 ~ Children in family room ~ Dogs allowed in bar and bedrooms ~ Open 11–3, 6.30(7 in winter)–11; 12–3, 7–10.30 Sun; closed 25 Dec evening ~ Bedrooms: /£42(£46S)

TARRANT MONKTON

Langton Arms *Village signposted from A354, then head for church*

Pretty 17th-c thatched pub owned by a farming couple, simple beamed bar with huge inglenook, interesting bar

food strong on tradition (and your dog may be lucky enough to be offered a free sausage), good real ales, no smoking bistro restaurant in attractively reworked barn; garden with very good wood-chip play area, good nearby walks
Free house ~ Licensees Barbara and James Cossins ~ Real ale ~ Bar food (all day Sat and Sun, not 25 Dec) ~ Restaurant ~ (01258) 830225 ~ Children welcome in family room and restaurant ~ Dogs allowed in bar and bedrooms ~ Open 11.30–11; 12–10.30 Sun ~ Bedrooms: £50B/£70B

WORTH MATRAVERS
Square & Compass *At fork of both roads signposted to village from B3069*
Hardly changed in the 90 years or more that this family has run it, good beers from hallway serving hatches, simple furniture on flagstones, woodburner, friendly locals and service, home-made pasties, collection of local fossils and artefacts; lovely peaceful hilltop setting, great view to the coast from front benches, good walks from the pub
Free house ~ Licensee Charlie Newman ~ Real ale ~ No credit cards ~ (01929) 439229 ~ Children welcome ~ Dogs welcome ~ Open 12–3, 6–11; 12–11 Sat; 12–3, 7–10.30 Sun; may close Sun evening winter

ESSEX

Dog Friendly Hotels and B&Bs

BURNHAM-ON-CROUCH White Harte *The Quay, Burnham-on-Crouch, Essex CM0 8AS (01621) 782106* **£59**; 19 rms, 11 with own bthrm. Old-fashioned 17th-c yachting inn on quay overlooking the River Crouch with its own jetty; high ceilings, oak tables, polished parquet flooring, sea pictures, panelling, residents' lounge, and decent food in bar and restaurant; dogs welcome in bedrooms

Dog Friendly Pubs

CHAPPEL
Swan *Wakes Colne; pub visible just off A1124 Colchester-Halstead*
Spacious low-beamed rambling bar with lots of dark tables for diners, very big fireplace (filled with lots of plants in summer), good value popular food with daily fresh dish, good drinks choice, cheery helpful staff; sheltered heated courtyard, garden with River Colne running through towards an impressive Victorian viaduct
Free house ~ Licensee Terence Martin ~ Real ale ~ Bar food (12–2.30(3 Sun), 7(6.30 Sat)–10.30) ~ Restaurant ~ (01787) 222353 ~ Children in eating area of bar and restaurant ~ Dogs allowed in bar ~ Open 11–3, 6–11; 11–11 Sat; 12–10.30 Sun

FULLER STREET
Square & Compasses *From A12 Chelmsford–Witham take Hatfield Peverel exit, and from B1137 there follow Terling signpost, keeping straight on past Terling towards Great Leighs; from A131 Chelmsford–Braintree turn off in Great Leighs towards Fairstead and Terling*
Small civilised country pub with cheerily individualistic licensees, welcoming atmosphere, and wide choice of good interesting food; L-shaped beamed bar with rustic decorations and big log fires, good drinks, gentle country views from tables outside
Free house ~ Licensees Howard Potts and Ginny Austin ~ Real ale ~ Bar food (12–2, 7–9(10 Fri–Sat); light snacks at any time)

~ Restaurant ~ (01245) 361477 ~ Well behaved children welcome in eating area of the bar ~ Dogs welcome ~ Open 11.30–3, 6.30(7 in winter)–11; 12–3, 7–10.30 Sun; closed Mon

HORNDON-ON-THE-HILL

Bell M25 junction 30 into A13, then left into B1007 after 7 miles, village signposted from here

Bustling heavily beamed bar with high-backed settles, flagstones, polished oak boards, very good prettily presented food, good wines and beers, warmly welcoming feel; very attractive beamed bedrooms

Free house ~ Licensee John Vereker ~ Real ale ~ Bar food (12–1.45, 6.45–9.45; not bank hols) ~ Restaurant ~ (01375) 642463 ~ Children in eating area of bar and restaurant ~ Dogs allowed in bar and bedrooms ~ Open 11–2.30(3 Sat), 5.30(6 Sat)–11; 12–4, 7–10.30 Sun; closed 25, 26 Dec ~ Bedrooms: /£65B

GLOUCESTERSHIRE

Dog Friendly Hotels and B&Bs

BIBURY Bibury Court Bibury, Cirencester, Gloucestershire GL7 5NT (01285) 740337 **£125**, plus special breaks; 18 individual rms. Lovely peaceful mansion dating from Tudor times, in beautiful gardens, with an informal friendly atmosphere, panelled rooms, antiques, huge log fires, conservatory, a fine choice of breakfasts, and good interesting food; cl Christmas and New Year; disabled access; dogs welcome in bedrooms

CHELTENHAM Hotel on the Park *Evesham Rd, Cheltenham, Gloucestershire GL52 2AH (01242) 518898* **£118.50**, plus special breaks; 12 lovely rms. Warmly welcoming and handsome Regency house with elegantly furnished drawing room and dining room, pretty flowers and antiques, and imaginative food in stylish restaurant – good breakfasts, too; children over 8; dogs by special arrangement

CHELTENHAM Kanninsky Hotel *Bayshill Road, Cheltenham, Gloucestershire GL50 3AS (01242) 527788* **£110.90**; 48 large, stylish and well equipped rms. White-painted Regency hotel with an interesting mix of old and new furnishings, antiques and modern paintings, big pot plants, lots of mirrors, unusual collections on walls, tiled or wooden floors, and a relaxed, informal atmosphere; enjoyable modern food in bustling Café Paradiso, friendly bar, willing young staff, basement nightclub, and seats out on decked terrace; they are kind to families; dogs anywhere

CHIPPING CAMPDEN Eight Bells *Church St, Chipping Campden, Gloucestershire GL55 6JG (01386) 840371* **£70**, plus winter breaks; 6 rms. Neatly restored heavy-beamed 14th-c pub by church, with a newly refurbished bar, three log fires, interesting food with fresh local produce, friendly staff, decent wines and beers, a new terrace, and pleasant courtyard; cl 25 Dec; dogs anywhere

CLEARWELL Tudor Farmhouse *Clearwell, Coleford, Gloucestershire GL16 8JS (01594) 833046* **£70**, plus special breaks; 22 cottagey rms. Carefully restored Tudor farmhouse and stone cottages with landscaped gardens and surrounding fields; lots of beams, oak doors and sloping floors, delicious food in candlelit restaurant, and friendly staff; cl Christmas; disabled access; dogs welcome away from restaurant

CORSE LAWN Corse Lawn House *Corse Lawn, Gloucester GL19 4LZ (01452) 780771* **£125**, plus special breaks; 19 pretty, individually furnished rms. Magnificent Queen Anne building with comfortable and attractive day rooms, a distinguished restaurant with imaginative food and excellent wines (there's a less pricey bistro-style operation too), warmly friendly staff, a relaxed atmosphere, and an indoor swimming pool, tennis court, croquet, and horses in 12 acres of surrounding gardens and fields; cl 24–26 Dec; disabled access; dogs welcome away from restaurant

GREAT RISSINGTON Lamb *Great Rissington, Cheltenham, Gloucestershire GL54 2LP (01451) 820388* **£55***, plus special breaks; 14 pretty rms – several at higher price are suites with own lounge. Civilised 17th-c inn with a bustling and friendly atmosphere and nice mix of customers in the cosy bar, some interesting things to look at such as part of a propeller from a Wellington bomber that crashed in the garden in 1943, a residents' lounge with log fire, enjoyable bar food and a more extensive choice in no smoking restaurant, seats in the sheltered hillside garden, and good nearby walks; disabled access; dogs welcome in bedrooms

GUITING POWER Guiting Guest House *Post Office Lane, Guiting Power, Cheltenham, Gloucestershire GL54 5TZ (01451) 850470* **£70**; 7 pretty rms with thoughtful extras. 16th-c Cotswold stone guest house with inglenook fireplaces, beams, and rugs on flagstones, two sitting rooms, enjoyable Aga-cooked food, attentive owners, and a very relaxed atmosphere; cl Christmas week; dogs in one room

HAZLETON Windrush House *Hazleton, Cheltenham, Gloucestershire GL54 4EB (01451) 860364* **£51**; 4 rms, 2 with own bthrm. Warmly friendly and neatly kept no smoking guest house, with exceptionally good imaginative food, lovely breakfasts, log fire, and traditional furnishings; cl mid-Dec to Feb; no children; dogs welcome

PAINSWICK Painswick Hotel *Kemps Lane, Painswick, Stroud, Gloucestershire GL6 6YB (01452) 812160* **£125**, plus special breaks; 19 well equipped comfortable rms. 18th-c Palladian mansion – once a grand rectory – with fine views, antiques and paintings in the elegant rooms, open fires, good food using the best local produce, a thoughtful wine list, and a relaxed, friendly atmosphere; garden with croquet lawn; they are kind to families; dogs welcome in bedrooms

PARKEND Edale House *Folly Rd, Parkend, Lydney, Gloucestershire GL15 4JF (01594) 562835* **£51**, plus special breaks; 5 rms. Georgian house opposite cricket green and backing on to Nagshead Nature Reserve; comfortable, homely sitting room, little bar, very good food in attractive no smoking dining room (overlooking the garden), and a relaxed atmosphere; cl New Year; children over 12; dogs welcome

ST BRIAVELS George *St Briavels, Lydney, Gloucestershire GL15 6TA (01594) 530228* **£55**; 4 rms. Pleasant old pub in particularly interesting village overlooking 12th-c castle, with three rambling rooms, big stone fireplace, a Celtic coffin lid dating from 1070 (found in a fireplace here and now mounted next to the bar counter), cosy dining room, real ales, and good food; outdoor chessboard; dogs may be accepted

STOW-ON-THE-WOLD Old Stocks *The Square, Stow-on-the-Wold, Cheltenham, Gloucestershire GL54 1AF (01451) 830666* **£80**, plus special breaks; 18 rms. Well run 16th/17th-c Cotswold stone hotel with cosy welcoming small bar, beams and open fire, comfortable residents'

lounge, good food, friendly staff, and sheltered garden; cl 18–28 Dec; disabled access; dogs welcome away from restaurant

THORNBURY Thornbury Castle *Castle St, Thornbury, Bristol BS35 1HH (01454) 281182* **£185**; 25 opulent rms, some with big Tudor fireplaces or fine oriel windows. Impressive and luxuriously renovated early 16th-c castle with antiques, tapestries, huge fireplaces and mullioned windows in the baronial public rooms, three dining rooms (one in the base of a tower), fine cooking, extensive wine list (inc wine from their own vineyard), thoughtful friendly service, and vast grounds inc the oldest Tudor gardens in England; cl 4 days Jan; partial disabled access; dogs allowed at discretion of manager

WINSTONE Winstone Glebe *Winstone, Cirencester, Gloucestershire GL7 7JU (01285) 821451* **£60**; 3 rms. Small Georgian rectory in quiet countryside with five acres of gardens and paddocks, tennis, and lots of surrounding walks; friendly hosts, traditional furnishings, and delicious food (by arrangement); cl Christmas; dogs by arrangement

Dog Friendly Pubs

BISLEY

Bear *Village signposted off A419 just E of Stroud*
Elegantly gothic 16th-c former courthouse with meandering L-shaped bar, enjoyable home-made bar food, well kept real ales, sheltered little flagstoned courtyard, comfortable bedrooms; steep stone-built village in attractive hilly country *Pubmaster ~ Tenants Simon and Sue Evans ~ Real ale ~ Bar food (not Sun evening) ~ (01452) 770265 ~ Children in family room ~ Dogs welcome ~ Occasional Weds evening jazz ~ Open*

11.30–3, 6–11; 12–3, 7–10.30 Sun ~ Bedrooms: I/£40

CHEDWORTH

Seven Tuns *Village signposted off A429 NE of Cirencester; then take second signposted right turn and bear left towards church*

Good mix of walkers, cyclists, locals and diners in bustling 17th-c pub with antique prints in comfortable lounge, public bar opening into no smoking dining room, log fires throughout, enjoyable bar food, good drinks choice, prompt service; plenty of outside tables, some by waterwheel and stream

Youngs ~ Tenant Kevin Dursley ~ Real ale ~ Bar food (all day in summer; 11–2.30, 6–10 in winter) ~ (01285) 720242 ~ Children welcome ~ Dogs welcome ~ Open 11–11; 12–10.30 Sun; 11–3, 6–11 in winter

LOWER ODDINGTON

Fox *Near Stow-on-the-Wold*

Smart restauranty pub under new owners, with fresh flowers, flagstones and an inglenook fire, good interesting food and wines, tables on a heated terrace, and cottagey garden; a good eight-mile walk starts from here, though a stroll around the pretty village might be less taxing

Free house ~ Licensees Sally and Kirk Ritchie ~ Real ale ~ Bar food (till 10pm) ~ Restaurant ~ (01451) 870555 ~ Children welcome if quiet and well behaved ~ Dogs allowed in bedrooms ~ Open 12–3, 6.30–11; 12–3, 7–10.30 Sun; closed 25 Dec, evenings 26 and 31 Dec, 1 Jan ~ Bedrooms: I/£75S(£85B)

NAILSWORTH

Weighbridge *B4014 towards Tetbury*

Three cosily old-fashioned rooms with black beams, stripped stone walls, antique settles and country chairs, black rustic ironware, rustic tables in upper hayloft, enjoyable food majoring on popular 2 in1 pies, good drinks choice, friendly chatty licensees; picnic-sets out in sheltered landscaped garden

Free house ~ Licensees Jane and Simon Hudson ~ Real ale ~ Bar food (all day) ~ (01453) 832520 ~ Children in restaurant ~ Dogs welcome ~ Open 12–11; 12–10.30 Sun

OLD SODBURY

Dog *Not far from M4 junction 18: A46 N, then A432 left towards Chipping Sodbury*

Bustling two-level bar with stripped stone, low beams, timbering and open fires, huge choice of food, big garden with lots of seating, summer barbecues and play area; new bedrooms in former skittle alley

Whitbreads ~ Lease John and Joan Harris ~ Real ale ~ Bar food (11–10; 12–3, 7–9.30 Sun) ~ (01454) 312006 ~ Children in eating area of bar ~ Dogs allowed in bedrooms ~ Open 11–11; 12–10.30 Sun ~ Bedrooms: £26(£45B)/£40(£60B)

SAPPERTON

Bell *Village signposted from A419 Stroud–Cirencester; OS Sheet 163, map reference 948033*

Emphasis on very good food using local produce, good wines and local ales too, cosy rooms with flagstones and log fires; Harry the springer spaniel likes to greet everyone; tables prettily set outside, good surrounding walks, and horses have their own tethering rail

Free house ~ Licensees Paul Davidson and Pat Le Jeune ~ Real ale ~ Bar food (not Mon except bank hols) ~ Restaurant ~ (01285) 760298 ~ Children allowed but under 10 to leave by 6.30 ~ Dogs welcome ~ Open 11–2.30, 6.30–11; 12–3, 7–10.30 Sun

HAMPSHIRE

Dog Friendly Hotels and B&Bs

CHERITON Flower Pots *Cheriton, Alresford, Hampshire SO24 0QQ (01962) 771318* **£60**; 5 rms. Unspoilt and quietly comfortable village local run by very friendly family, with two pleasant little bars, log fire, decent bar food, super own-brew beers, and old-fashioned seats on the pretty lawns; no credit cards; cl Christmas and New Year; children over 12; dogs welcome

HURSTBOURNE TARRANT Esseborne Manor *Hurstbourne Tarrant, Andover, Hampshire SP11 0ER (01264) 736444* **£120***, plus special breaks; 15 individually decorated rms. Small stylish Victorian manor with a calm relaxed atmosphere, comfortable lounge and snug little bar, good modern cooking, log fires in elegant dining room, and friendly staff; neat gardens with tennis, and croquet; special arrangement with local golf club and health and leisure centre; disabled access; dogs welcome in bedrooms

LYMINGTON Efford Cottage *Milford Rd, Everton, Lymington, Hampshire SO41 0JD (01590) 642315* **£55**, plus winter breaks; 3 comfortable rms. Spacious Georgian cottage nr New Forest, and in an acre of garden, with marvellous breakfasts inc home baked bread and home-made jams and preserves, enjoyable evening meals using home-grown produce (only as part of winter special breaks), and good parking; no children; dogs by arrangement and away from dining room

LYMINGTON Stanwell House *High St, Lymington, Hampshire SO41 9AA (01590) 677123* **£110***, plus special breaks; 29 pretty rms. Handsome town house with comfortable attractively furnished lounge, cosy little bar, good imaginative food, and pretty walled back garden; 50-ft yacht for charter; dogs welcome

LYNDHURST Poussin at Parkhill *Beaulieu Rd, Lyndhurst, Hampshire SO43 7FZ (023) 8028 2944* **£110**, plus special breaks; 19 carefully furnished, spacious and comfortable rms. 18th-c former hunting lodge reached by a long drive through wood-flanked New Forest pastures; a nice, informal, family-run atmosphere, big welcoming peaceful lounge/hall with sofas, easy chairs, a writing desk, a good log fire and daily papers, and an inner hall with a grand piano and longcase clock; the pink-carpeted lounge has another big log fire, lots of sofas and deep easy chairs and low tables, and big windows looking over a narrow flagstoned terrace and pond-side lawn; a little library with lots of books, smallish cosy bar, and pretty, formal restaurant with conservatory-style extension; quite excellent, beautifully presented food, a good wine list with an exceptionally good choice of wines by the glass, and enjoyable breakfasts with home-preserved fruits and home-made jams and marmalade; dogs in one bedroom only

MIDDLE WALLOP Fifehead Manor *Middle Wallop, Stockbridge, Hampshire SO20 8EG (01264) 781565* **£130**w, plus special breaks; 17 spacious rms, some in the garden wing. Friendly and comfortable old brick manor house in several acres of lovely gardens; a restful atmosphere, pleasant small lounge and bar, fine food in candlelit restaurant, enjoyable breakfasts, and friendly staff; croquet; disabled access; dogs in garden rooms

MILFORD ON SEA Westover Hall *Park Lane, Milford-on-Sea, Lymington, Hampshire SO41 0PT (01590) 643044* **£145***, 12 individually furnished rms, 6 with fine views.

Victorian mansion in marvellous spot nr peaceful beach, views of Christchurch Bay, Isle of Wight and the Needles rocks; impressive original features inc dramatic stained glass, magnificent oak panelling, and ornate ceilings, very good food using the best local produce in grand (but not stuffy) candlelit restaurant overlooking garden and sea, lighter lunches in lounge bar also with water views, sunny terrace, and helpful friendly staff; dogs welcome in bedrooms

OWER Ranvilles Farm House *Pauncefoot Hill, Romsey, Hampshire SO51 6AA (023) 80 814481* **£55***; 3 attractively decorated rms with antique furniture. Dating from the 13th c when Richard de Ranville came from Normandy and settled with his family, this Grade II* listed house is in five quiet acres of gardens and paddock, with warmly friendly owners and enjoyable breakfasts; no evening meals; cl 25 and 31 Dec, 1 Jan; disabled access; dogs welcome in bedrooms

SPARSHOLT Lainston House *Sparsholt, Winchester, Hampshire SO21 2LT (01962) 863588* **£150**, plus wknd breaks; 50 spacious, individually decorated rms. Close to Winchester, this elegant William and Mary hotel stands in 63 acres of fine parkland, with tennis court, croquet, fishing, archery, and clay pigeon shooting; fresh flowers and paintings in relaxing, elegant lounge, panelled bar and restaurant, a fine wine list, and good British cooking; gym; disabled access; dogs in some ground floor rooms

Dog Friendly Pubs

BURSLEDON

Jolly Sailor *2 miles from M27 junction 8; then A27 towards Sarisbury, then just before going under railway bridge turn right towards Bursledon Station; it's best to park round here and walk as the lane up from the station is now closed to cars*

Lovely spot overlooking the River Hamble, airy front bar with ship pictures, beamed and flagstoned back bar with pews and settles by huge fireplace, plenty of tables outside, enjoyable bar food and good choice of drinks

Badger ~ Managers Adrian Jenkins and Jackie Cosens ~ Real ale ~ Bar food (12–9.30) ~ (023) 8040 5557 ~ Children in no smoking area ~ Dogs allowed in bar ~ Open 11–11; 12–10.30 Sun; closed 25 Dec

CRAWLEY

Fox & Hounds *Village signposted from A272 and B3420 NW of Winchester*

Curiously and charmingly Swiss-looking pub in an attractive village, beams and candlelight, three log fires, relaxed atmosphere, helpful friendly staff, very good food using fresh local produce, good drinks; summer garden barbecues

Free house ~ Licensees Richard and Kathryn Crawford ~ Real ale ~ Bar food (12–2, 6–9(9.30 Fri–Sat) ~ Restaurant ~ (01962) 776006 ~ Children in eating area of bar ~ Dogs welcome ~ Open 11–3, 6–11; 12–3, 6–10.30 Sun; closed 25 Dec

FRITHAM

Royal Oak *Village signed from exit roundabout, M27 junction 1; quickest via B3078, then left and straight through village; head for Eyeworth Pond*

Charming and cheerfully welcoming thatched New Forest

pub, part of a working farm, with restored panelling, beams and oak flooring in three neat and nicely traditional rooms, roaring log fires, simple lunchtime food (evening meals Mon or by arrangement), good real ales, big garden with wknd barbecues, hog roasts and lovely views; fine surrounding walks.

Free house ~ Licensees Neil and Pauline McCulloch ~ Real ale ~ Bar food (lunchtime – though see text) ~ No credit cards ~ (023) 8081 2606 ~ Children welcome but must be well behaved ~ Dogs welcome ~ Occasional local folk ~ Open 11–3, 6–11; 11–11 Sat; 12–10.30 Sun

HAWKLEY

Hawkley Inn *Take first right turn off B3006, heading towards Liss ¾ mile from its junction with A3; then after nearly two miles take first left turn into Hawkley village – Pococks Lane; OS Sheet 186, map reference 746292*

Half-a-dozen interesting real ales, their own cider, a chatty, friendly atmosphere, simple décor with big pine tables, promptly served tasty bar food; pleasant garden with climbing frame, pub on Hangers Way Path

Free house ~ Licensee Al Stringer ~ Real ale ~ Bar food (not Sun evening) ~ (01730) 827205 ~ Well behaved children in eating area of bar until 8pm ~ Dogs welcome ~ Live music every second winter Sat ~ Open 12–2.30(3 Sat), 6–11; 12–3, 7–10.30 Sun

LANGSTONE

Royal Oak *High Street (marked as cul-de-sac – actually stops short of the pub itself); village is last turn left off A3023 (confusingly called A324 on some signs) before Hayling Island bridge*

Great spot with boats arriving at high tide, or wading birds when the tide is out, spacious flagstoned bar with simple furnishings on parquet and ancient flagstones, two open fires, decent bar food with two linked dining areas looking over the water; good coastal paths nearby

Whitbreads ~ Manager Simon Courtley ~ Real ale ~ Bar food (12–2.30, 6–9; snacks served all day) ~ Restaurant ~ (023) 9248 3125 ~ Children in eating area of bar and restaurant ~ Dogs allowed in bar ~ Folk club 3rd Sun of month ~ Open 11–11; 12–10.30 Sun

NORTH GORLEY

Royal Oak *Ringwood Road; village signposted off A338 S of Fordingbridge*

Relaxed 17th-c thatched pub with particularly friendly helpful staff, neatly refurbished no smoking lounge, pews, old engravings and corner woodburner in main bar with steps down to attractive L-shaped eating area, good bar food, neatly kept sheltered back garden with play area; nearby duck pond and roaming ponies

Whitbreads ~ Lease David Catt ~ Real ale ~ Bar food (12–2, 6–9) ~ Restaurant ~ (01425) 652244 ~ Children in restaurant and family room ~ Dogs welcome ~ Open 11–11; 12–10.30 Sun

OVINGTON

Bush *Village signposted from A31 on Winchester side of Alresford*

Charming little low-ceilinged cottage with garden by the River Itchen, nice old-fashioned décor, quickly served good (if not cheap) food; friendly Scottish springer spaniel called Paddy

Wadworths ~ Managers Nick and Cathy Young ~ Real ale ~ Bar food (not Sun evening) ~ (01962) 732764 ~ Well behaved children in eating area of bar until 9 ~ Dogs welcome ~ Open 11–3, 6–11; 12–2.30, 7–10.30 Sun; closed 25 Dec

TICHBORNE

Tichborne Arms *Village signed off B3047*

Neat thatched pub near Wayfarers Walk and Itchen Way, many fine walks; panelling, latticed windows, log fire, interesting Tichborne Case memorabilia, popular food and two pub dogs; picnic-sets out in big well kept garden, no children inside
Free house ~ Licensees Keith and Janie Day ~ Real ale ~ Bar food (12–1.45, 6.30–9.45) ~ (01962) 733760 ~ Dogs welcome ~ Open 11.30–2.30, 6–11; 12–3, 7–10.30 Sun; closed evenings 25 and 26 Dec and evening 1 Jan

HEREFORDSHIRE

Dog Friendly Hotels and B&Bs

BRIMFIELD Roebuck *Brimfield, Ludlow, Shropshire SY8 4NE (01584) 711230* **£70***; 3 rms. Smart country dining pub with an impressive inglenook fireplace in the quiet, old-fashioned locals' snug, two other civilised bars with small open fires, a cosy no smoking dining room, super stylish food, well kept real ales, carefully chosen wines, and caring staff; dogs welcome in bedrooms
FOWNHOPE Green Man *Fownhope, Hereford HR1 4PE (01432) 860243* **£69.50***, plus special breaks; 20 rms. Attractive Tudor inn with impressive oak-beamed lounge (the residents' lounges are no smoking), log fire, and generously served popular bar food; adjoining leisure club with large swimming pool, solarium, spa, sauna and gym; partial disabled access; dogs in bedrooms and bar area
HOARWITHY Old Mill *Hoarwithy, Hereford, Herefordshire HR2 6QH (01432) 840602* **£42**; 6 cottagey rms. Cream-

painted 18th-c building with the mill-race flowing through the flower-filled garden; log fire and books in beamed sitting room, good breakfasts and enjoyable evening meals, friendly helpful owners, and lots to do nearby; no smoking; disabled access; dogs allowed if well behaved

LEDBURY Feathers *25 High St, Ledbury, Herefordshire HR8 1DS (01531) 635266* **£95**, plus special breaks; 19 carefully decorated rms making the most of the old beams and timbers. Very striking, mainly 16th c, black and white hotel with a relaxed atmosphere, log fires, comfortable lounge hall with country antiques, beams and timbers, particularly enjoyable food and friendly service in hop-decked Fuggles bar, a good wine list, and a fine mix of locals and visitors; health and leisure spa with indoor swimming pool; dogs welcome

ROSS-ON-WYE Brookfield House *Over Ross St, Ross-on-Wye, Herefordshire HR9 7AT (01989) 562188* **£45**, plus special breaks; 8 rms, some with own bthrm. Part Queen Anne and part Georgian house with sunny terrace and little garden, and a view over the town; welcoming owners, log fire in lounge, and super breakfasts in big airy room; cl Christmas; children over 8; dogs welcome

Dog Friendly Pubs

AYMESTREY
Riverside Inn *A4110; N off A44 at Mortimer's Cross, W of Leominster*
Attractively placed timbered dining pub with log fires, antiques and stripped pine in rambling beamed bar, big restaurant area, good ambitious food, good drinks and service; tables out by river and in steep tree-sheltered

garden, comfortable bedrooms (free taxi service for residents to start of the Mortimer Trail)
Free house ~ Licensees Richard and Liz Gresko ~ Real ale ~ Bar food ~ Restaurant ~ (01568) 708440 ~ Children welcome ~ Dogs welcome ~ Open 11–11; 12–10.30 Sun; 11–3, 6–11; 12–3, 7–10.30 Sun in winter; closed 25 Dec ~ Bedrooms: £90S(£90B)/£65B

BRIMFIELD
Roebuck Inn *Village signposted just off A49 Shrewsbury–Leominster*
Smart country dining pub with imaginative though not cheap food using local produce and daily fresh fish, good drinks choice, courteous welcoming staff, quiet old-fashioned locals' snug with impressive inglenook, 15th-c oak-panelled main bar, light and airy bow-windowed third bar and brightly decorated airy dining room; terrace tables, nice bedrooms, good breakfast
Free house ~ Licensees David and Sue Willson-Lloyd ~ Real ale ~ Bar food ~ Restaurant ~ (01584) 711230 ~ Children in eating area of bar ~ Dogs allowed in bar and bedrooms ~ Open 11.30–2.30, 6.30–11; 12–3, 7–10.30 Sun ~ Bedrooms: £45B/£70S(£70B)

CRASWALL
Bulls Head *Hay-on-Wye–Llanfihangel Crucorney road along Golden Valley, via Longtown; OS Sheet 161, map reference 278360*
Welcoming stone-built pub in a remote peaceful spot between the Golden Valley and the Black Mountains, ideal for walking – and the kind of place where the helpful landlord will happily make you a packed lunch to take on your walk; unpretentious low-beamed bar like a farmhouse kitchen, with good hatch-served beers, well prepared

inventive food (huge helpings), tables outside, a play area and room for camping

Free house ~ Licensee Paul Chicken ~ Real ale ~ Bar food ~ (01981) 510616 ~ Dogs welcome ~ Open 11–11 Mon–Sat; 11–5 Sun; closed Sun evening, all Mon and Tues ~ Bedrooms: £30(£40B)/£45(£50B)

TITLEY

Stagg *B4355 N of Kington*

Deceptively simple-looking old place focusing on beautifully prepared food using local supplies of the best fresh often organic ingredients for both the pubbier blackboard menu (not available Sat evening or Sun lunchtime) and the more elaborate main menu, good wines and other drinks, friendly enthusiastic staff; the bar, though comfortable and hospitable, is not large; tables outside

Free house ~ Licensees Steve and Nicola Reynolds ~ Real ale ~ Bar food (till 10 Mon–Sat) ~ Restaurant ~ (01544) 230221 ~ Children welcome ~ Dogs allowed in bar and bedrooms ~ Open 12–3, 6.30–11(7–10.30 Sun); closed Mon (except bank hols then closed Tues), May Day bank hol, 26 Dec, 1 Jan and first two wks in Nov ~ Bedrooms: £40S(£40B)/£60S(£60B)

ISLE OF WIGHT

Dog Friendly Hotels and B&Bs

BONCHURCH Lake Hotel *Bonchurch, Ventnor, Isle of Wight PO38 1RF (01983) 852613* **£62.50***, plus special breaks; 20 rms. Early 19th-c country house in two acres of pretty gardens, 400 metres from beach; lots of flowers and plants in three light and airy lounges (one is an attractive conservatory), a well stocked bar, and enjoyable food in neat restaurant; cl Dec–Feb; children over 3; partial disabled access; dogs welcome in bedrooms

SEAVIEW Priory Bay Hotel *Priory Croft, Priory Rd, Seaview, Isle of Wight PO34 5BU (01983) 613146* **£148**, plus special breaks; 18 individually furnished rms with 9 more in cottages. Former Tudor farmhouse with Georgian and more recent additions in grounds leading to a fine sandy private beach with a beach bar (good for lunch); lovely day rooms with comfortable sofas, books and magazines on coffee tables, pretty flower arrangements, imaginative food in restaurant with charming Georgian murals and elaborate plasterwork, and an informal, relaxed atmosphere; outdoor swimming pool, tennis, croquet, and a nine-hole par three golf course; disabled access; dogs in cottages in grounds

SEAVIEW Seaview Hotel *High St, Seaview, Isle of Wight PO34 5EX (01983) 612711* **£80**, plus special breaks; 16 attractively decorated rms, some with sea views and private drawing rooms. Small, friendly and spotlessly kept hotel with fine ship photographs in the chatty and relaxed front dining bar, an interesting old-fashioned back bar, good imaginative bar food, and a highly regarded evening restaurant; cl 3 days over Christmas; proper high tea for children (must be over 5 in evening restaurant); partial disabled access; dogs welcome in bedrooms

VENTNOR Royal Hotel *Belgrave Rd, Ventnor, Isle of Wight PO38 1JJ (01983) 852186* **£130**; 55 well equipped rms. Friendly Victorian hotel with fine sea views, neat gardens with heated outdoor pool, spacious and comfortable day rooms, cosy candlelit bar with open fire, good food in attractive restaurant, and helpful service; disabled access; dogs welcome in bedrooms

YARMOUTH George Hotel *Quay St, Yarmouth, Isle of Wight PO41 0PE (01983) 760331* **£165**; 17 comfortable rms. 17th-c house by the harbour, with gardens leading to little private beach; a fine flagstoned hall, fresh flowers and open fires, a convivial bar and attractive residents' sitting room with marvellously relaxing atmosphere, imaginative enjoyable food in informal brasserie and smart restaurant, hearty breakfasts, and prompt courteous service; motor yacht for hire; children over 10; dogs welcome in bedrooms

Dog Friendly Pubs

BONCHURCH
Bonchurch Inn *Bonchurch Shute; from A3055 E of Ventnor turn down to Old Bonchurch opposite Leconfield Hotel*
Welcoming old Italian-run stone pub spread around a central courtyard, furniture-packed Victorian bar, food inc several Italian dishes; holiday flat for up to six people
Free house ~ Licensees Ulisse and Gillian Besozzi ~ Real ale ~ Bar food ~ Restaurant ~ (01983) 852611 ~ Children in separate family room ~ Dogs allowed in bar and bedrooms ~ Open 11–3, 6.30–11; 12–3, 7–10.30 Sun; closed 25 Dec ~ Bedrooms: /£70B

KENT

Dog Friendly Hotels and B&Bs

BOUGHTON LEES Eastwell Manor *Eastwell Park, Boughton Lees, Ashford, Kent TN25 4HR (01233) 219955* **£200**, plus special breaks; 62 prettily decorated rms in both hotel and 19 courtyard cottages (some cottages have their own garden and can also be booked on self-catering basis). Fine Jacobean-style manor (actually rebuilt in the 1920s) in 62 acres with croquet lawn, tennis court, two boules pitches and putting green; grand oak-panelled rooms, open fires, comfortable leather seating, antiques and fresh flowers, courteous helpful service, and extremely good food; health and fitness spa with 20-metre indoor pool and 14 treatment rooms, and lots of walks; disabled access; dogs welcome in bedrooms

CANTERBURY Cathedral Gate *36 Burgate, Canterbury, Kent CT1 2HA (01227) 464381* **£88**, plus special breaks; 27 rms, 12 with own bthrm and some overlooking cathedral. 15th-c hotel that predates the adjoining sculpted cathedral gateway; bow windows, massive oak beams, sloping floors, antiques and fresh flowers, continental breakfast in little dining room or your own room, and a restful atmosphere; municipal car parks a few minutes away; dogs welcome but bring own bedding

PLUCKLEY Elvey Farm *Pluckley, Ashford, Kent TN27 0SU (01233) 840442* **£65.50***; 9 rms, some in the oast house roundel, some in original barn and stable block. 15th-c farmhouse in secluded spot on 75-acre working family farm, with timbered rooms, inglenook fireplace, and French windows from lounge on to sun terrace; ample play areas for children; cl Christmas; disabled access; dogs welcome in bedrooms

Dog Friendly Pubs

BROOKLAND

Woolpack *On A259 from Rye, as you approach Brookland, take the first right turn where the main road bends left, just after the expanse of Walland Marsh; OS Sheet 189, map reference 977244*

Crooked early 15th-c cottage in the marshes, with smuggling history, floors of quarry tiles or uneven bricks, black pine panelling, low beams, informal mix of furnishings, roaring log fire in massive inglenook fireplace, friendly staff and pub cat, good value enjoyable straightforward bar food

Shepherd Neame ~ Tenants John and Pat Palmer ~ Real ale ~ Bar food ~ (01797) 344321 ~ Children in family room ~ Dogs welcome ~ Open 11–3, 6–11; 12–3, 7–10.30 Sun

CHIDDINGSTONE

Castle Inn *Village signposted from B2027 Tonbridge–Edenbridge*

It's worth a walk around the National Trust village to look at the picturesque cluster of unspoilt Tudor houses, and the countryside around here is pleasant too; carefully modernised handsome beamed bar, prettily set tables outside, straightforward daytime menu with more elaborate evening dishes, impressive wine list

Free house ~ Licensee Nigel Lucas ~ Real ale ~ Bar food (11–9.30) ~ Restaurant ~ (01892) 870247 ~ Children welcome (not in public bar) ~ Dogs welcome ~ Open 11–11; 12–10.30 Sun

PLUCKLEY
Dering Arms *Pluckley Station, which is signposted from B2077*
Former hunting lodge with entirely home-made food majoring on fresh fish, stylishly plain high-ceilinged main bar with roaring log fire, good wine list, friendly accommodating service
Free house ~ Licensee James Buss ~ Real ale ~ Bar food ~ Restaurant ~ (01233) 840371 ~ Children in eating area of bar, family room and restaurant ~ Dogs allowed in bar and bedrooms ~ Open 11.30–3, 6–11; 12–3, 7–10.30 Sun; closed 26–27 Dec ~ Bedrooms: £30/£40

LANCASHIRE

Dog Friendly Hotels and B&Bs

ASHWORTH VALLEY Leaches Farm *Ashworth Rd, Rochdale, Lancashire OL11 5UN (01706) 41117* **£42***; 3 rms, shared bthrm. Creeper-clad 17th-c hill farm with really wonderful views, massive stone walls, beams and log fires; cl 22 Dec–2 Jan; children over 8; dogs by arrangement
BILSBORROW Guy's Thatched Hamlet *St Michael's Rd, Bilsborrow, Preston, Lancashire PR3 0RS (01995) 640010* **£42***, plus wknd breaks; 53 smartly modern rms. Bustling complex of thatched buildings by the canal, comprising a restaurant and pizzeria, a tavern, and the accommodation part, Guy's Lodgings; craft shops and outside entertainment, a play area, all-weather cricket pitch, and crown green

bowling; a useful base for exploring the area; open all day; cl 25 Dec; disabled access; dogs welcome in bedrooms

BLACKPOOL Imperial Hotel *North Promenade, Blackpool, Lancashire FY1 2HB (01253) 623971* **£110**, plus special breaks; 181 well equipped pretty rms, many with sea views. Fine Victorian hotel overlooking the sea, with spacious and comfortable day rooms, lots of period features, enjoyable food and fine wines, and a full health and fitness club with indoor swimming pool, gym, sauna and so forth; children's club during summer, Christmas and Easter; lots to do nearby; disabled access; dogs welcome in bedrooms

BROMLEY CROSS Last Drop Village Hotel *Hospital Rd, Bromley Cross, Bolton, Lancashire BL7 9PZ (01204) 591131* **£105**; 128 rms. Big well equipped hotel complex cleverly integrated into olde-worlde pastiche village complete with stone-and-cobbles street of gift and teashops, bakery, etc, even a spacious creeper-covered pub with lots of beamery and timbering, popular one-price hot and cold buffet, and heavy tables out on attractive flagstoned terrace; disabled access; dogs welcome in bedrooms

CAPERNWRAY New Capernwray Farmhouse *Capernwray, Carnforth, Lancashire LA6 1AD (01524) 734284* **£66**; 3 comfortable rms. Pretty 300-year-old ex-farmhouse with helpful friendly owners, cosy lounge, stone walls and beams, and candlelit dinner in what was the dairy with an informal house-party atmosphere; cl Nov–Feb; children over 9; dogs welcome in bedrooms

CHIPPING Gibbon Bridge Hotel *Green Lane, Chipping, Preston, Lancashire PR3 2TQ (01995) 61456* **£100**, plus special breaks; 29 spacious individual rms, inc 22 split-level suites, most with views of the Bowland Hills. Country hotel on the edge of the Forest of Bowland, with beautiful landscaped gardens (plus a popular bandstand which can be used for civil weddings or for music events), and old-fashioned values of quality and personal service; attractively presented food using home-grown produce in airy restaurant and adjoining conservatory, a quiet relaxing atmosphere, and fine wines; health and gym area; a good base for walking and short driving trips; good disabled access; dogs in two restricted bedrooms

COWAN BRIDGE Hipping Hall *Cowan Bridge, Kirkby Lonsdale, Carnforth, Lancashire LA6 2JJ (01524) 271·187* **£96**, plus special breaks; 7 pretty rms, 5 in main hotel, 2 cottage suites across courtyard (with self-catering facilities). Relaxed country-house atmosphere and delicious food in handsome small hotel with help-yourself drinks in conservatory, an open fire, a lovely beamed Great Hall with minstrels' gallery, and four acres of walled gardens; small antiques/curios shop, fine walks from front door; cl 22 Dec–14 Jan; dogs in cottage suites

HURST GREEN Shireburn Arms *Whalley Rd, Hurst Green, Clitheroe, Lancashire BB7 9QJ (01254) 826518* **£70**, plus special breaks; 18 rms, several refurbished this year. Lovely 17th-c country hotel with a refined but friendly atmosphere, an airy and newly redecorated modernised bar, comfortable lounge, open fires, well presented enjoyable food in newly refurbished restaurant, good service, and fine view of the Ribble Valley from the conservatory; disabled access; dogs welcome in bedrooms

WADDINGTON Backfold Cottage *The Square, Waddington, Clitheroe, Lancashire BB7 3JA (01200) 422367* **£50***; 3 rms. Tiny 17th-c cottage in cobbled street, attractive millennium clock on the front, beautiful antique furnishings (inc a doll's house in the lounge); very good service, all-day snacks, and candlelit evening meals (bring your own wines); nearby walks; children at owner's discretion; dogs welcome in bedrooms

Dog Friendly Pubs

CONDER GREEN
Stork *3 miles from M6 junction 33: A6 towards Lancaster, first left, then fork left; just off A588*
In a fine spot where the River Conder joins the Lune estuary and handy for the estuary path, with tables outside looking over the bleak marshes; bustling rambling panelled rooms, good winter fire, generous popular bar food, good bedrooms
Free house ~ Licensee Tony Cragg ~ Real ale ~ Bar food (all day Sun) ~ Restaurant ~ (01524) 751234 ~ Children welcome ~ Dogs allowed in bar and bedrooms ~ Open 11–11; 12–10.30 Sun; closed 25 Dec ~ Bedrooms: £27S/£44S

LITTLE ECCLESTON
Cartford *Cartford Lane, off A586 Garstang–Blackpool, by toll bridge*
Popular for reasonably priced enjoyable food, and particularly strong on beer, with an attractive rambling interior, pleasantly uncoordinated cosy seating areas, good log fire, friendly obliging service, and nicely relaxed atmosphere; tables outside with a play area, good bedrooms, and walks by the River Wyre (tidal here)
Own brew ~ Licensees Andrew Mellodew and Val Williams ~ Real ale ~ Bar food (12–9 Sun) ~ Restaurant ~ (01995) 670166 ~ Children welcome ~ Dogs welcome ~ Open 12–3, 6.30(7 Mon–Thurs in winter)–11; 12–10.30 Sun ~ Bedrooms: £36.95B/£48.95B

WHITEWELL

Inn at Whitewell *Most easily reached by B6246 from Whalley;
road through Dunsop Bridge from B6478 is also good*

Outstanding inn deep in the Forest of Bowland, surrounded
by wooded rolling hills set off against higher moors,
impressive old-fashioned and antique furnishings, roaring log
fires, courteous friendly staff, very good bar food inc coffee
and cream teas all day, picnic hampers if you're staying in one
of the excellent bedrooms, fine choice of drinks, pleasant
suntrap garden, miles of private fishing

*Free house ~ Licensee Richard Bowman ~ Real ale ~ Bar food
(12–2, 7.30–9.30) ~ Restaurant ~ (01200) 448222 ~ Children
welcome ~ Dogs welcome ~ Open 11–3, 6–11; 12–2, 7–11
Sun ~ Bedrooms: £78B/£108B*

LEICESTERSHIRE AND RUTLAND

Dog Friendly Hotels and B&Bs

EMPINGHAM White Horse *Main St, Empingham,
Oakham, Rutland LE15 8PR (01780) 460221* **£65***, plus
special breaks; 13 pretty rms, some in a delightfully
converted stable block. Attractive, bustling old inn, handy
for Rutland Water; a relaxed and comfortable atmosphere,
a big log fire and fresh flowers in open-plan lounge, big
helpings of very enjoyable food inc fine breakfasts, coffee
and croissants from 8am, and cream teas all year; attractive
no smoking restaurant, well kept real ales, and efficient
friendly service; cots/high chairs; cl 25 Dec; good disabled
access; dogs welcome in bedrooms

OAKHAM Whipper-In *Market Pl, Oakham, Rutland LE15 6DT (01572) 756971* **£84**, plus special breaks; 24 rms. Attractive and well run 17th-c stone coaching inn with oak-beamed and panelled lounge opening into cosy eating area, log fires, good food in cosy restaurant, and well kept ales; disabled access; dogs welcome in bedrooms

ROTHLEY Rothley Court *Westfield Lane, Rothley, Leicester LE7 7LG (0116) 237 4141* **£105**; 32 rms (the ones in the main house have more character). Mentioned in the Domesday Book, this carefully run manor house with its beautifully preserved 13th-c chapel has some fine oak panelling, open fires, a comfortable bar, conservatory, and courteous staff; seats out on the terrace and in the garden; disabled access; dogs welcome in bedrooms

STAPLEFORD Stapleford Park *Stapleford, Melton Mowbray, Leicestershire LE14 2EF (01572) 787522* **£246.75***; 51 individually designed rms, plus cottage. Luxurious country house, extravagantly restored, in lovely large grounds with riding and stabling, tennis, croquet, putting green, 18-hole championship golf course, trout fishing, falconry, and clay-pigeon shooting; lots of mahogany, opulent furnishings, fine oil paintings and an impressive library, delicious restaurant food, enthusiastic American owner, and warmly welcoming staff; health spa and indoor swimming pool; cots/babysitting; disabled access; dogs welcome away from restaurant

UPPINGHAM Lake Isle *16 High St East, Uppingham, Oakham, Rutland LE15 9PZ (01572) 822951* **£108**, plus special breaks; 12 rms with home-made biscuits, sherry and fresh fruit, and three cottage suites. In a charming market town, this 18th-c restaurant-with-rooms has an open fire in the attractive lounge, a redecorated bar (once a barber's where the schoolboys had their hair cut), good, imaginative food in refurbished restaurant (enjoyable breakfasts, too), a carefully chosen wine list, and a small and pretty garden; dogs welcome in bedrooms

Dog Friendly Pubs

EXTON
Fox & Hounds *Signposted off A606 Stamford–Oakham*
Handsome former coaching inn on picturesque tree-lined green, handy for Viking Way and Rutland Water; civilised and comfortable high-ceilinged lounge bar, much pubbier locals' bar, attentive staff, generous nicely prepared bar food; tables out on pleasant back lawn
Free house ~ Licensees David and Jennifer Hillier ~ Real ale ~ Bar food ~ Restaurant ~ No credit cards ~ (01572) 812403 ~ Children in eating area of bar and restaurant ~ Dogs allowed in bar and bedrooms ~ Open 11–3, 6.30–11; 12–3, 7–10.30 Sun ~ Bedrooms: £24/£38

LINCOLNSHIRE

Dog Friendly Hotels and B&Bs

LINCOLN D'Isney Place *Eastgate, Lincoln LN2 4AA (01522) 538881 £86*, plus special breaks; 17 charming rms.* Friendly 18th-c hotel with lovely gardens (one wall of the cathedral close forms its southern boundary), a relaxed and homely atmosphere, good breakfasts using free-range eggs served on bone china in your room (there are no public rooms), and friendly owners; partial disabled access; dogs welcome

STAMFORD George *71 St Martins, Stamford, Lincolnshire PE9 2LB (01780) 750700* **£105**, plus special breaks; 47 individually decorated rms. Ancient former coaching inn with a quietly civilised atmosphere, sturdy timbers, broad flagstones, heavy beams and massive stonework, and open log fires; good food in Garden Lounge, restaurant and courtyard (in summer), an excellent range of drinks inc very good value Italian wines, and welcoming staff; well kept walled garden and sunken croquet lawn; disabled access; dogs welcome in bedrooms

WINTERINGHAM Winteringham Fields *1 Silver St, Winteringham, Scunthorpe, Lincolnshire DN15 9ND (01724) 733096* **£105**; 10 pretty, chintzy rms with period furniture (3 off courtyard). Thoughtfully run restaurant-with-rooms in 16th-c manor house with comfortable and very attractive Victorian furnishings, beams and open fires, really excellent, inventive and beautifully presented food (inc a marvellous cheeseboard) in no smoking dining room, fine breakfasts, exemplary service, and an admirable wine list; cl 2 wks Christmas, last wk Mar, 1st wk Aug, last wk Oct; disabled access; babes in arms and children over 8; dogs welcome in bedrooms

Dog Friendly Pubs

ASWARBY
Tally Ho *A15 S of Sleaford (but N of village turn-off)*
Handsome 17th-c house with two log fires and chunky candlelit pine tables in chatty bar, generous enjoyable bar food, good house wines, attractive no smoking pine-furnished

restaurant; tables out behind, among the fruit trees, comfortable bedrooms in neatly converted back block

Free house ~ Licensees Christine and Peter Robertson ~ Real ale ~ Bar food (12–2.30, 6.30–10) ~ Restaurant ~ (01529) 455205 ~ Children in eating area of bar and restaurant ~ Dogs welcome ~ Open 12–3, 6–11(7–10.30 Sun) ~ Bedrooms: £35B/£50B

SOUTH WITHAM

Blue Cow *Village signposted just off A1 Stamford– Grantham (with brown sign for pub)*

A good A1 stop for car-weary dogs, beams and flagstones, good value family food from all-day sandwiches up, good real ales brewed on the spot, tables out on pleasant terrace; we still haven't heard from anyone who has stayed here, but they will even stable your horse overnight

Own brew ~ Licensees Dick and Julia Thirlwell ~ Real ale ~ Bar food (12–2.30, 6–9.30) ~ Restaurant ~ (01572) 768432 ~ Children in eating area of bar, restaurant and family room ~ Dogs allowed in bar and bedrooms ~ Open 12–11 ~ Bedrooms: £40S/£45S

NORFOLK

Dog Friendly Hotels and B&Bs

BLAKENEY Blakeney Hotel *Blakeney, Holt, Norfolk NR25 7NE (01263) 740797* **£144**, plus special breaks; 59 very comfortable rms, many with views over the salt marshes and some with own little terrace. Overlooking the harbour with fine views, this friendly hotel has comfortable and appealing public rooms, good food, very pleasant staff, indoor swimming pool, saunas, spa bath, billiard room, and safe garden; very well organised for families, with plenty to do for them nearby; good disabled access; dogs welcome in bedrooms

BURNHAM MARKET Hoste Arms *Market Pl, Burnham Market, King's Lynn, Norfolk PE31 8HD (01328) 738777* **£96**, plus special breaks; 36 comfortable rms. Handsome inn on green of lovely Georgian village, with a smartly civilised atmosphere, attractive bars (the main bar has been renovated this year), some interesting period features, big log fires, conservatory lounge, stylish food (plus morning coffee and afternoon tea), well kept real ales and good wines, and professional friendly staff; big new awning covering a sizeable eating area in the garden; partial disabled access; dogs welcome

MORSTON Morston Hall *The Street, Morston, Holt, Norfolk NR25 7AA (01263) 741041* **£190** inc dinner, plus special breaks; 6 comfortable rms with country views. Attractive 17th-c flint-walled house in tidal village, with lovely quiet gardens, two small lounges, one with an antique fireplace, a conservatory, and hard-working friendly young owners; particularly fine modern English cooking (they also run cookery demonstrations and hold wine and food events), a thoughtful small wine list, and super breakfasts; croquet; cl Jan; dogs welcome away from public rooms; they are kind to families; cl 1 Jan–1 Feb; partial disabled access; dogs welcome in bedrooms

MUNDFORD Crown *Crown St, Mundford, Thetford, Norfolk IP26 5HQ (01842) 878233* **£55**; 14 good rms. Friendly small village pub, originally a hunting inn and rebuilt in the 18th c, with an attractive choice of reasonably priced straightforward food, very welcoming staff, a happy atmosphere, and well kept real ales; disabled access; dogs welcome

SWAFFHAM Strattons *Ash Close, Swaffham, Norfolk PE37 7NH* (01760) 723845 **£100***, plus special breaks; 7 interesting, pretty rms. No smoking and environment-friendly Palladian-style villa run by charming warmly friendly owners with comfortable individually decorated drawing rooms, family photographs, paintings, lots of china cats (and several live ones), antiques, patchwork throws, fresh and dried flowers, and open fires; delicious highly imaginative food using local (and home-grown) organic produce, a carefully chosen wine list illustrated with Mrs Scott's own watercolours, and super breakfasts; big cupboard full of toys and games for children; garden with croquet; cl Christmas; dogs welcome

THORNHAM Lifeboat *Ship Lane, Thornham, Hunstanton, Norfolk PE36 6LT* (01485) 512236 **£84**, plus special breaks; 13 pretty rms, most with sea view. Rambling old white-painted stone pub, well placed by coastal flats, with lots of character in the main bar – open fires, antique oil lamps, low settles and pews around carved oak tables, big oak beams hung with traps and yokes, and masses of guns, swords and antique farm tools; several rooms lead off; enjoyable popular food in bar and elegant restaurant and well kept real ales; sunny conservatory with steps up to terrace with seats and playground; marvellous surrounding walks; children welcomed rather than tolerated; partial disabled access; dogs welcome away from eating areas

THORPE MARKET Elderton Lodge *Cromer Rd, Thorpe Market, Norwich NR11 8TZ* (01263) 833547 **£115**, plus special breaks; 11 rms. 18th-c shooting lodge for adjacent

Gunton Hall, with lots of original features, fine panelling, a relaxing lounge bar with log fire, an airy conservatory where breakfast and lunch are served, and Langtry Restaurant with good food using fresh fish and game; six acres of mature grounds overlooking herds of deer; children over 6 or under a year; partial disabled access; dogs welcome away from restaurant

TITCHWELL Titchwell Manor Hotel *Main Rd, Titchwell, King's Lynn, Norfolk PE31 8BB (01485) 210221* **£70**, plus special breaks; 16 light, pretty rms. Comfortable hotel, handy for nearby RSPB reserve, with an open fire, magazines and good naturalists' records of the wildlife, a cheerful bar, attractive no smoking brasserie restaurant (lots of seafood) with French windows on to sheltered neatly kept walled garden, and particularly helpful licensees and staff; lots of walks and footpaths nearby; high tea for younger children; disabled access; dogs welcome

WARHAM Three Horseshoes *The Street, Warham, Wells-next-the-Sea, Norfolk NR23 1NL (01328) 710547* **£52**; 5 rms, one with own bthrm. Basic but cheerful local with marvellously unspoilt traditional atmosphere in its three friendly gaslit rooms, simple furnishings, a log fire, very tasty generous bar food, decent wines, home-made lemonade, and very well kept real ales; bedrooms are in the Old Post Office adjoining the pub, with lots of beams and a residents' lounge dominated by an inglenook fireplace; cl 25–26 Dec; no children; dogs welcome

WINTERTON-ON-SEA Fishermans Return *The Lane, Winterton-on-Sea, Great Yarmouth, Norfolk NR29 4BN (01493) 393305* **£70***; 3 rms. Traditional 300-year-old pub in quiet village, close to the beach, with warmly welcoming owners, a relaxed lounge bar, open fire, good home-made food inc fresh fish (fine crabs in season), enjoyable break-fasts, and sheltered garden with children's play equipment; dogs welcome

Dog Friendly Pubs

CLEY NEXT THE SEA
Three Swallows *Off A149 E of Blakeney; in village, turn into Holt Road and head for church at Newgate Green*
Cheery village local, handy for the salt marshes and a favourite with bird-watchers; unpretentious pubby bar with good log fire and elaborately carved bar counter, small family eating area, second log fire in informal no smoking stripped pine restaurant, good value generous quickly served food, perhaps wandering tabby cats; big pretty garden with popular summer barbecues, climbing frame, budgerigars and goat pen; simple comfortable bedrooms, good breakfast
Pubmaster ~ Tenants Jean and James Walker ~ Real ale ~ Bar food (12–2, 6–9; all day weekends) ~ (01263) 740526 ~ Children in restaurant and family room ~ Dogs welcome ~ Open 11–11; 12–10.30 Sun ~ Bedrooms: £35B/£49B

REEPHAM
Old Brewery House *Market Square; B1145 W of Aylsham*
Georgian hotel with good pubby atmosphere and lots of farming and fishing bric-a-brac in big high-ceilinged bar, red-carpeted panelled lounge leading off, decent bar food, picnic-sets on front terrace, back gardens with water features
Free house ~ Licensee David Peters ~ Real ale ~ Bar food ~ Restaurant ~ (01603) 870881 ~ Children welcome ~ Dogs allowed in bar and bedrooms ~ Open 11–11; 12–10.30 Sun ~ Bedrooms: £47.50B/£75B

NORTHAMPTONSHIRE

Dog Friendly Hotels and B&Bs

BADBY Windmill *Main St, Badby, Daventry, Northamptonshire NN11 3AN (01327) 702363* **£72**, plus special breaks; 8 rms. Carefully modernised and warmly welcoming thatched stone inn with beams, flagstones and huge inglenook fireplace in front bar, a cosy comfortable lounge, a relaxed and civilised atmosphere, good generously served bar and restaurant food, and decent wines; fine views of the pretty village from car park; disabled access; dogs welcome in bedrooms

CRANFORD Dairy Farm *12 St. Andrews Lane, Cranford, Kettering, Northamptonshire NN14 4AQ 01536 330273* **£50**; 4 comfortable rms. Charming 17th-c manor house of great character on an arable and sheep farm, with oak beams and inglenook fireplaces, antiques and family paintings, good homely cooking using home-grown fruit and vegetables, kind, attentive owners, and garden with charming summer house; no smoking; dogs by arrangement

OLD Wold Farm *Harrington Rd, Old, Northampton, Northamptonshire NN6 9RJ (01604) 781258* **£50**; 5 rms. No smoking 18th-c farmhouse in a quiet village, with spacious interesting rooms, antiques and fine china, hearty breakfasts in the beamed dining room, attentive welcoming owners, snooker table, and two pretty gardens; dogs welcome in bedrooms

OUNDLE Talbot *New St, Oundle, Peterborough, Cambridgeshire PE8 4EA (01832) 273621* **£95**, plus special breaks; 39 most attractive rms. Mary, Queen of Scots walked to her execution down a staircase that's now in this carefully refurbished 17th-c hotel; attractive cosy lounge, big log fire, good food in timbered restaurant, and garden; dogs welcome in bedrooms

NORTHUMBRIA

Dog Friendly Hotels and B&Bs

ALNMOUTH Marine House Hotel *1 Marine Rd, Alnmouth, Alnwick, Northumberland NE66 2RW (01665) 830349* **£78**, plus special breaks; 11 rms. 17th-c stone hotel by golf links, with fine sea views; log fire and plenty of books in traditional upstairs residents' lounge, cosy bar, and enjoyable freshly prepared food in cheerfully decorated no smoking dining room; self-catering also; cl Jan; children over 7; dogs welcome

CHOLLERFORD George *Chollerford, Hexham, Northumberland NE46 4EW (01434) 681611* **£125**, plus special breaks; 47 well equipped rms. Quiet hotel with fine gardens sloping down to the river, and the 17th-c bridge over North Tyne visible from the candlelit restaurant; thoughtful attentive service; swimming pool and leisure club; fishing, putting green, and mountain bike hire; limited disabled access; dogs welcome in bedrooms

CORNHILL-ON-TWEED Tillmouth Park *Cornhill-on-Tweed, Northumberland TD12 4UU (01890) 882255* **£130**, plus special breaks; 14 spacious, pretty rms with period furniture. Solid stone-built country house in 15 acres of parkland, with comfortable relaxing lounges, open fires, a galleried hall, good food in bistro or restaurant, and a carefully chosen wine list; fishing, nearby golf, and shooting; lots to do nearby; dogs welcome in bedrooms

CROOKHAM Coach House *Crookham, Cornhill-on-Tweed, Northumberland TD12 4TD (01890) 820293* **£54***; 9 individual rms with fresh flowers and nice views, 7 with own bthrm. 17th-c farm buildings around a sunny courtyard, with helpful and friendly long-serving owner, an airy beamed lounge with comfortable sofas and big arched windows, good breakfasts with home-made preserves (which you can also take home), afternoon tea, and enjoyable dinners using own-grown vegetables; lots to do nearby; cl 31 Oct–Easter; good disabled access; dogs welcome in bedrooms

DURHAM Durham Marriott Royal County *Old Elvet, Durham, Co Durham DH1 3JN (0191) 386 6821* **£125**, plus special breaks; 150 attractive well equipped rms. In the city centre with views of the castle and cathedral, this extended and newly refurbished hotel has original Tudor beams, panelling and an unusual stained-glass ceiling, a convivial lounge area, airy conservatory, two restaurants, and good leisure facilities; disabled access; dogs welcome in bedrooms

GATESHEAD Eslington Villa *8 Station Rd, Low Fell, Gateshead, Tyne & Wear NE9 6DR (0191) 487 6017* **£69.50**, plus wknd breaks; 18 rms. Comfortable, extended Edwardian house in quiet residential area with some original features, a lounge with comfortably modern furniture and bay windows overlooking garden, good food in conservatory restaurant, and a friendly atmosphere; cl bank hols and Christmas; disabled access; dogs welcome in bedrooms

GRETA BRIDGE Morritt Arms *Greta Bridge, Barnard Castle, County Durham DL12 9SE (01833) 627232* **£83.50**, plus special breaks; 23 rms. Smartly old-fashioned coaching inn where Dickens stayed in 1838 to research for *Nicholas*

Nickleby – one of the interesting bars has a colourful Dickensian mural; comfortable lounges, fresh flowers, good open fires, and pleasant garden; coarse fishing; pets allowed; attractive garden with children's play area; disabled access; dogs welcome away from bistro and restaurant

HEADLAM Headlam Hall *Headlam, Darlington, County Durham DL2 3HA (01325) 730238* **£87**, plus special breaks; 36 pretty rms, in the main house and adjacent coach house, plus 2-bedroom cottage in village. Peaceful Jacobean mansion in four acres of carefully kept gardens with little trout lake, tennis court, and croquet lawn; elegant rooms, a fine carved oak fireplace in the main hall, stylish food in the four individually decorated rooms of the restaurant, and courteous staff; indoor swimming pool, snooker and sauna, and gym; cl 25 Dec; disabled access; dogs welcome in bedrooms

LONGFRAMLINGTON Embleton Hall *Longframlington, Morpeth, Northumberland NE65 8DT (01665) 570249* **£85**; 13 comfortable, pretty and individually decorated rms. Charming hotel in lovely grounds surrounded by fine countryside, with a particularly friendly relaxed atmosphere and courteous staff; neat little bar, elegant lounge, log fires, excellent value bar meals, and very good food in the attractive dining room; disabled access; dogs welcome in bedrooms

LONGHORSLEY Linden Hall *Longhorsley, Morpeth, Northumberland NE65 8XF (01670) 516611* **£128**, plus special breaks; 50 individually decorated rms. Georgian hotel in 450 acres of landscaped park with clay pigeon shooting, mountain biking (bike hire available), 18-hole golf course, pitch and putt, croquet, lots of leisure facilities inc a big swimming pool, and health and beauty treatments; pubby bar, elegant drawing room, and good food in attractive restaurant; children in main restaurant early evening only; disabled access; dogs welcome in bedrooms

ROMALDKIRK Rose & Crown *Romaldkirk, Barnard Castle, County Durham DL12 9EB (01833) 650213* **£90**, plus special breaks; 12 rms – those in the main house have lots of character. Smart and interesting old coaching inn by green of delightful Teesdale village, with Jacobean oak settle, log fire, old black and white photographs, and lots of brass in the beamed traditional bar; cosy residents' lounge, very good imaginative food in bar and fine oak-panelled restaurant, and well kept real ales and wines; cl Christmas; disabled access; dogs welcome in bedrooms

STANNERSBURN Pheasant *Stannersburn, Hexham, Northumberland NE48 1DD (01434) 240382* **£65***, plus special breaks; 8 rms. Beautifully located unpretentious 17th-c stone inn close to Kielder Water and its quiet forests; traditional, comfortable lounge, simple public bar, a happy mix of customers, good food inc excellent fresh veg and enjoyable Sun lunch, well kept real ales, a fine choice of malts, good welcoming service, and nice breakfasts; picnic-sets in streamside garden; cl 25–26 Dec; disabled access; dogs welcome in bedrooms

Dog Friendly Pubs

BLANCHLAND
Lord Crewe Arms *B6306 S of Hexham*
Partly 13th-c inn with cloister garden, striking crypt bar and other rooms reeking of history; decent bar food, and the lovely old stone village is separated from the rest of the world by miles of moorland
Free house ~ Licensees A Todd, Peter Gingell and Ian Press,

Lindsey Sands ~ Real ale ~ Bar food ~ Restaurant ~ (01434) 675251 ~ Children welcome ~ Dogs welcome ~ Open 11–11.30; 12–10.30 Sun ~ Bedrooms: £80B/£110B

CARTERWAY HEADS

Manor House Inn *A68 just N of B6278, near Derwent Reservoir*

Enticing choice of good food, welcoming helpful young staff, oak pews and pine tables in locals' bar, comfortable lounge with woodburner, picture-window views over moorland pastures, good beers, wines, farm cider and malt whiskies; rustic tables outside, comfortable bedrooms with good breakfasts

Free house ~ Licensees Moira and Chris Brown ~ Real ale ~ Bar food (all day Fri–Sun and bank hols) ~ Restaurant ~ (01207) 255268 ~ Well behaved children welcome ~ Dogs allowed in bar and bedrooms ~ Open 11–11; 12–10.30 Sun; closed 25 Dec evening ~ Bedrooms: £33B/£55B

NEWTON-BY-THE-SEA

Ship *Village signposted off B1339 N of Alnwick; Low Newton – paid parking 200 metres up road on right, just before village (none in village)*

Plainly furnished beamed pub tucked into top corner of charming seaside cottage square by long broad beach and off-shore seal rocks, hospitable service, enjoyable lunchtime snacks and (must book) appealing evening meals using fresh local produce, tables outside

Free house ~ Licensee Christine Forsyth ~ Bar food (12–2, 7–8(not Tues–Thurs evenings in winter; not Sun or Mon evenings) ~ (01665) 576262 ~ Children welcome ~ Dogs welcome ~ Open 11–11; 12–3, 9(7 Fri)–11 winter wkdays, 11–4, 6.30–11 winter Sat, 12–4, 8–10.30 winter Sun; closed Mon Nov–Feb

THROPTON
Three Wheat Heads B6341
Stone-built 17th-c Coquetdale hotel, attractive garden with play area and lovely views towards the Simonside Hills, good fires in comfortable bar (with elaborate grandfather clock) and roomy dining area, emphasis on the enjoyable food, friendly efficient staff; good bedrooms

Pubmaster ~ Lease Danny Scullion ~ Real ale ~ Bar food (12–2, 6–9; 12–9 Sat and Sun) ~ Restaurant ~ (01669) 620262 ~ Children welcome ~ Dogs allowed in bar and bedrooms ~ Open 11–3, 6–11; 11–11 Sat; 11–10.30 Sun ~ Bedrooms: £39B/£59S(£59B)

NOTTINGHAMSHIRE

Dog Friendly Hotels and B&Bs

LANGAR Langar Hall *Church Lane, Langar, Nottingham, Nottinghamshire NG13 9HG (01949) 860559* **£130***, plus special breaks; 10 lovely rms, some in wing and courtyard as well. Fine country house in spacious grounds with beautifully furnished elegant rooms, pillared dining hall with paintings for sale, antiques and fresh flowers, a relaxed informal atmosphere, a lively and friendly owner, and very good food; quite a few facilities for children; disabled access; dogs welcome in bedrooms

NOTTINGHAM Lace Market *29–31 High Pavement, Nottingham, Nottinghamshire NG1 1HE (0115) 852 3232* **£120.90**; 29 modern, comfortable rms. Next to a lovely church, this Georgian town house has a relaxed atmosphere, friendly young staff, a convivial bar with daily papers, wood-strip floors and strong but subtle colours, good brasserie-style food in contemporary restaurant, and enjoyable breakfasts; dogs welcome in bedrooms

OXFORDSHIRE

Dog Friendly Hotels and B&Bs

BURFORD Lamb *Sheep St, Burford, Oxfordshire OX18 4LR (01993) 823155* **£120**, plus special breaks; 15 rms. Very attractive 500-year-old Cotswold inn with lovely restful atmosphere, spacious beamed, flagstoned and elegantly furnished lounge, classic civilised public bar, bunches of flowers on good oak and elm tables, three winter log fires, antiques, imaginative food in airy restaurant, and pretty little walled garden; cl 25–26 Dec; dogs welcome away from dining room

CLIFTON Duke of Cumberlands Head *Clifton, Banbury, Oxfordshire OX15 0PE (01869) 338534* **£70**; 6 rms in sympathetic extension. Pretty thatched 17th-c stone inn with a friendly atmosphere, very good food in bar and no smoking back restaurant, enjoyable breakfasts, log fire, well kept beers and wines, and helpful service; tables in garden; dogs welcome

HORTON-CUM-STUDLEY Studley Priory *Horton-cum-Studley, Oxford OX33 1AZ (01865) 351203* **£165**, plus special breaks; 18 rather luxurious rms. Once a Benedictine nunnery, this lovely Elizabethan manor stands in 13 wooded acres; fine panelling, 16th- and 17th-c stained-glass windows, antiques, big log fires, and good sofas and armchairs in the elegant drawing room and cosy bar, smartly uniformed friendly service, and seasonally changing menus in attractive high-beamed restaurant, hung with lots of landscape prints; grass tennis court and croquet; dogs welcome in bedrooms

KINGHAM Mill House *Station Rd, Kingham, Chipping Norton, Oxfordshire OX7 6UH (01608) 658188* **£110**, plus special breaks; 23 good rms with country views. Carefully renovated 17th-c flour mill in seven acres with trout stream; comfortable spacious lounge, open log fire in lounge bar, original features such as two bread ovens, a cosy popular restaurant, and very good interesting food; disabled access; dogs welcome in bedrooms

KINGSTON BAGPUIZE Fallowfields *Southmoor, Kingston Bagpuize, Abingdon, Oxfordshire OX13 5BH (01865) 820416* **£150***, plus special breaks; 10 rms. Delightful Gothic-style manor house with elegant, relaxing sitting rooms, open fires, good imaginative food using home-grown produce in attractive conservatory dining room, courteous helpful service, and 12 acres of pretty gardens and paddocks; tennis court; no smoking; lots to see nearby; cl 24–25 Dec; dogs welcome in bedrooms

MOULSFORD Beetle & Wedge *Ferry Lane, Moulsford, Wallingford, Oxfordshire OX10 9JF (01491) 651381* **£175**, plus special breaks; 10 pretty rms, most with a lovely river view. Civilised riverside hotel where Jerome K Jerome wrote *Three Men in a Boat* and where H G Wells lived for a time (it was the Potwell in *The History of Mr Polly*); informal old beamed Boathouse Bar and lovely conservatory dining room (both with wonderful food – but must book), a carefully chosen wine list, open fires, fresh flowers, a riverside terrace and waterside lawn with moorings; nice walks; they are kind to families; disabled access; dogs welcome in bedrooms

OXFORD Randolph *Beaumont St, Oxford OX1 2LN* (01865) 247481 **£170**, plus special breaks; 114 rms. Fine neo-Gothick Victorian hotel facing the Ashmolean Museum; elegant comfortable day rooms, grand foyer, graceful restaurant with lovely plasterwork ceiling, and cellar wine bar; disabled access; dogs welcome in bedrooms

SHILLINGFORD Shillingford Bridge Hotel *Shillingford Rd, Shillingford, Wallingford, Oxfordshire OX10 8LZ* (01865) 858567 **£110**, plus special breaks; 42 rms. Riverside hotel with own river frontage, fishing and moorings, spacious comfortable bars and attractive airy restaurant (all with fine views), squash, outdoor heated swimming pool, and Sat dinner-dance; disabled access; dogs welcome away from restaurant

SHIPTON-UNDER-WYCHWOOD Shaven Crown *High St, Shipton-under-Wychwood, Chipping Norton, Oxfordshire OX7 6BA* (01993) 830330 **£95**, plus special breaks; 8 comfortable rms. Densely beamed, ancient stone hospice built around striking medieval courtyard with old-fashioned seats on cobbles, lily pool and roses; impressive medieval hall with a magnificent lofty ceiling, sweeping stairway and old stone walls, log fire in comfortable bar, intimate candlelit restaurant, well chosen wine list, good friendly service, warm relaxed atmosphere, and bowling green; children over 5 in evening dining room; disabled access; dogs welcome away from restaurant

STONOR Stonor Hotel *Stonor, Henley-on-Thames, Oxfordshire RG9 6HE* (01491) 638345 **£145***, plus special breaks; 11 individually decorated rms looking over intimate walled garden. Elegantly restored 18th-c coaching inn, with good imaginative food in charming conservatory restaurant and flagstoned Blades Bar; friendly staff; disabled access; dogs welcome in bedrooms

WOODSTOCK Feathers *Market St, Woodstock, Oxfordshire OX20 ISX* (01993) 812291 **£135**, plus special breaks; 20 individually decorated rms. Lovely old building with a fine relaxing drawing room and study, open fires, first-class friendly staff, a gentle atmosphere, daily-changing imaginative food inc lovely puddings, and a sunny courtyard with attractive tables and chairs; dogs welcome in bedrooms

Dog Friendly Pubs

SHENINGTON

Bell *Village signposted from A422 W of Banbury*

Ancient heavy-beamed golden stone pub in picturesque village, relaxed atmosphere, good wholesome food cooked by the landlady, tables outside; the West Highland terrier is called Lucy, the Labrador, Daisy, and the Great Dane, Oliver; good surrounding walks

Free house ~ Licensee Jennifer Dixon ~ Real ale ~ Bar food (not Mon lunchtime) ~ Restaurant ~ (01295) 670274 ~ Children in eating area of bar and restaurant ~ Dogs welcome ~ Open 12–2.30(3 Sat), 7–11; 12–3.30, 7–10.30 Sun; closed Mon lunchtime (except bank hols) ~ Bedrooms: £25/£50S

SWALCLIFFE

Stags Head *Bakers Lane, just off B4035*

Picturesque old thatched village pub, low beams, stripped stone, high-backed pews, oak floor and big woodburner, lighter second room with lots more tables, candles on them at night, enjoyable enterprising food, good drinks, welcoming licensees (they have two dogs and a cat); tables outside, nice garden with sensibly segregated play area, ducks and chickens *Free house ~ Licensees Ian and Julia Kingsford ~ Real ale ~ Bar food (12–2.15, 7–9.30; not Sun evening or Mon) ~ Restaurant ~ (01295) 780232 ~ Children in eating area of bar and restaurant ~ Dogs welcome ~ Open 11.30–2.30(3 Sat), 6.30–11; 12–4 Sun; closed Sun evening and all day Mon ~ Bedrooms: £35S/£60S*

SHROPSHIRE

Dog Friendly Hotels and B&Bs

CLUN New House Farm *Clun, Craven Arms, Shropshire SY7 8NJ* (01588) 638314 **£55***; 2 rms. Remote 18th-c farmhouse nr the Welsh border with plenty of surrounding hillside walks; no smoking homely rooms, packed lunches, good breakfasts, plenty of books, a country garden and peaceful farmland (which includes an Iron Age hill fort), and helpful friendly owner; cl end Oct–Easter; children over 10; dogs welcome in bedrooms

HOPTON WAFERS Crown *Hopton Wafers, Kidderminster, Worcestershire DY14 0NB* (01299) 270372 **£75**, plus special breaks; 7 rms. Attractive creeper-covered stone inn in pleasant countryside, with interestingly furnished bar, inglenook fireplace, enjoyable food, decent house wines, beers and malt whiskies, friendly efficient service, and streamside garden; children over 12; dogs welcome in bedrooms

KNOCKIN Top Farmhouse *Knockin, Oswestry, Shropshire SY10 8HN* (01691) 682582 **£48***; 3 pretty rms. Most attractive Grade I listed black and white timbered house dating back to the 16th c, with friendly owners, lots of timbers and beams, a log fire in the restful comfortable drawing room, good breakfasts in the large dining room, and an appealing garden; grand piano; children over 12; dogs welcome away from dining room

LONGVILLE Longville Arms *Longville, Much Wenlock, Shropshire TF13 6DT (01694) 771206* **£48***; 4 comfortable rms in converted stables, with showers. Warmly friendly inn with two spacious bars, well kept real ales, a wide range of enjoyable food in the new dining room, superb breakfasts, and a large terrace overlooking the big children's play area; disabled access; dogs welcome

LUDLOW Wheatsheaf *Lower Broad St, Ludlow, Shropshire SY8 1PQ (01584) 872980* **£45**, plus special breaks; 5 comfortable oak-beamed rms with showers. Attractively furnished small 17th-c pub built into medieval town gate; traditional atmosphere, two log fires, lots of hops, timbers, and exposed stone walls, wide range of good food in bar and no smoking restaurant (super steaks), and real ales; dogs welcome away from restaurant

NORTON Hundred House *Bridgnorth Rd, Norton, Shifnal, Shropshire TF11 9EE (01952) 730353* **£99**, plus special breaks; 10 cottagey rms with swing and lavender-scented sheets. Carefully refurbished mainly Georgian inn with quite a sophisticated feel, neatly kept bar with old quarry-tiled floors, beamed ceilings, oak panelling and handsome fireplaces, elaborate evening meals using inn's own herbs, friendly service, good bar food, and excellent breakfasts; delightful garden; dogs welcome in bedrooms

RHYDYCROESAU Pen-y-Dyffryn Hall *Rhydycroesau, Oswestry, Shropshire SY10 7JD (01691) 653700* **£90**, plus special breaks; 10 rms with really helpful information packs about where to go. Handsome Georgian stone-built rectory in five acres with lovely views of the Shropshire and Welsh hills, and trout fishing, hill-walking and riding (shooting can be arranged); log fires in both comfortable lounges, good food using the best local ingredients, helpful staff, and a relaxed friendly atmosphere; cl Jan; dogs welcome

STREFFORD Strefford Hall Farm *Strefford, Craven Arms, Shropshire SY7 8DE (01588) 672383* **£46***; 3 rms. No smoking Victorian stone-built farmhouse surrounded by 360 acres of working farm; woodburner in sitting room, good breakfasts, and lots of walks; cl Christmas and New Year; disabled access; dogs welcome in bedrooms

WORFIELD Old Vicarage *Hallon, Worfield, Bridgnorth, Shropshire WV15 5JZ (01746) 716497* **£130**, plus special breaks; 14 pretty rms. Restful and carefully restored Edwardian rectory in two acres; two airy conservatory-style lounges, very good interesting food in no smoking restaurant, a fine wine list, a cosseting atmosphere, and warmly friendly, helpful service; good disabled access; dogs welcome in bedrooms

WREKIN Buckatree Hall *Wrekin, Telford, Shropshire TF6 5AL (01952) 641821* **£85**, plus special breaks; 62 rms, several with own balconies and many with lake views. Comfortable former hunting lodge dating from 1820, in large wooded estate at the foot of the Wrekin; extended and modernised with comfortable day rooms, enjoyable food in the Terrace Restaurant, and helpful attentive service; dogs welcome in bedrooms

WROCKWARDINE Church Farm *Wrockwardine, Telford, Shropshire TF6 5DG (01952) 244917* **£58**; 6 individual well equipped rms, most with own bthrm. Friendly Georgian farmhouse on very ancient site overlooking the attractive garden and church; a relaxed atmosphere, particularly good caring service, beams and log fire in lounge, and good daily changing food in traditionally furnished dining room; children over 10; dogs welcome in bedrooms

Dog Friendly Pubs

BRIDGES
Horseshoe *Near Ratlinghope, below the W flank of the Long Mynd*
Comfortable and friendly old pub in picturesque setting among deserted hills in good walking country, good log fire, well kept beers and farm cider, decent straightforward bar food, tables out by the little River Onny
Free house ~ Licensee Colin Waring ~ Real ale ~ Bar food (12–3, 6–9; 12–9 Sat and Sun) ~ (01588) 650260 ~ Children welcome ~ Dogs welcome ~ Open 11–11; closed 25 Dec evening

HAMPTON LOADE
Lion *Off A442, 4½ miles S of Bridgnorth; look out for ducks on the pot-holed lane*
Charming 16th-c pub in delightful spot overlooking River Severn, two cosy and well worn bar rooms with roaring log fires, friendly helpful landlord, good beers, wines and local country wines (much used in the cooking), enjoyable bar food and imaginative evening restaurant dishes, quaint ferry crossing to Severn Valley Railway station opposite, lots of picnic-sets out on a big lawn
Free house ~ Licensee Rob Whittle ~ Real ale ~ Bar food (12–2, 7–9.30(10 Fri and Sat); 12–3(2.30 winter), 7–9 Sun) ~ Restaurant ~ (01746) 780263 ~ Children welcome if eating lunchtime or

booked evening ~ Dogs allowed in bar ~ Open 12–2.30, 7–11; 12–3.30(3 winter), 7–10.30 Sun; closed Mon except bank hols, 25 Dec and evening 26 Dec

SOMERSET

Dog Friendly Hotels and B&Bs

BARWICK **Little Barwick House** *Barwick, Yeovil, Somerset BA22 9TD* (01935) 423902 **£110**, plus special breaks; 6 attractive rms. Carefully run listed Georgian dower house in 3½ acres 2m S of Yeovil, and thought of as a restaurant-with-rooms; completely refurbished throughout this year but still with a lovely relaxed atmosphere, log fire in cosy lounge, excellent food using local produce, a thoughtful wine list, super breakfasts, nice afternoon tea, and particularly good service; cl Christmas, 2 wks Jan; dogs welcome in bedrooms

BATH **Royal Crescent Hotel** *16 Royal Crescent, Bath BA1 2LS* (01225) 823333 **£230**, plus special breaks; 45 luxurious rms. Elegant Georgian hotel in glorious curved terrace, with comfortable antique-filled drawing rooms, open fires and lovely flowers; imaginative modern cooking in Pimpernel Restaurant (in summer you can eat in the delightful garden), and impeccable service; plunge pool and croquet; they are kind to children; disabled access; dogs welcome

BECKINGTON **Pickford House** *Bath Road, Beckington, Frome, Somerset BA11 6SJ* (01373) 830329 **£38**; 5 rms with river view, some with balcony. Honey-coloured hilltop stone house, with open fire in sitting room, bar, delicious evening meals (by arrangement) and breakfasts, a relaxed friendly atmosphere, and helpful courteous owners; big garden with swimming pool; you can take over the house with a group of friends for a gourmet wknd; cl Christmas; partial disabled access; dogs welcome in bedrooms

HATCH BEAUCHAMP Farthings *Hatch Beauchamp, Taunton, Somerset TA3 6SG (01823) 480664* **£99**, plus special breaks; 10 spacious rms (inc a cottage suite) with thoughtful extras. Charming little Georgian house in three acres of gardens with helpful and hard-working long-serving owners, open fires in quiet lounge and convivial bar, and good varied food using fresh local produce; can arrange golf and other activities; children must be well behaved; dogs welcome in bedrooms

HOLFORD Combe House *Holford, Bridgwater, Somerset TA5 1RZ (01278) 741382* **£82**, plus special breaks; 16 rms. Warmly friendly former tannery (still has waterwheel) in a pretty spot, with comfortable rooms, log fires, good home-made food, and a relaxed atmosphere; heated indoor swimming pool and tennis court; cl mid-Nov–mid-Feb (but open Christmas and New Year); dogs welcome in bedrooms

HUNSTRETE Hunstrete House *Hunstrete, Pensford, Bristol BS39 4NS (01761) 490490* **£195**, plus special breaks; 25 individually decorated rms. Classically handsome, mainly 18th-c country-house hotel on the edge of the Mendips, in 92 acres inc lovely walled garden and deer park; comfortable and elegantly furnished day rooms with antiques, paintings, log fires, fresh garden flowers, a tranquil atmosphere, excellent service, and very good food using home-grown produce when possible; popular special events (wine tastings, jazz bands, champagne and horse racing);

new fitness room, croquet lawn, heated swimming pool, all-weather tennis court, and nearby riding; limited disabled access; dogs welcome in bedrooms

LUXBOROUGH Royal Oak *Luxborough, Watchet, Somerset TA23 0SH (01984) 640319* **£65**; 12 rms. Unspoilt and interesting old pub in idyllic spot, marvellous for exploring Exmoor; bar rooms with log fires in inglenook fireplaces, beams, flagstones, character furnishings and a thriving feel, three distinctive dining rooms (two no smoking), good food, and well liked breakfasts; dogs welcome away from dining rooms

SHEPTON MALLET Charlton House *Charlton Rd, Shepton Mallet, Somerset BA4 4PR (01749) 342008* **£155**; 16 attractive and stylish rooms with nice extras, and large bthrms. Substantial Georgian hotel in landscaped grounds; bare-boarded rooms with oriental rugs, dark red walls with lots of old photographs and posters, and show-casing the owners' Mulberry style of new-but-used look informal furnishings; smart dining room and 3-bay conservatory with lots of interesting plants and lovely flowers on the tables, exceptionally good modern cooking, beautifully presented, interesting wines, and helpful, efficient uniformed staff; seats on back terrace overlooking big lawn, unusual miniature moated castle as a water feature on the front lawn, and croquet; they are kind to children; dogs welcome in bedrooms

SOMERTON Lynch Country House *4 Behind Berry, Somerton, Somerset TA11 7PD (01458) 272316* **£49**; 8 prettily decorated rms, plus 3 extra in summer cottage. Carefully restored and homely Georgian house, with books in comfortable lounge, and good breakfasts (no evening meals) in airy room overlooking tranquil grounds and lake with black swans and exotic ducks; cl Christmas and New Year; dogs welcome in bedrooms

STOGUMBER Hall Farm *Station Rd, Stogumber, Taunton, Somerset TA4 3TQ (01984) 656321* **£40**; 6 rms. Old-fashioned B&B with optional evening meals (bring your own wine) — wonderfully unpretentious, with warmly friendly staff; cl Christmas and New Year; well behaved dogs welcome; cl Christmas and Jan; disabled access; dogs welcome in bedrooms

STOKE ST GREGORY Rose & Crown *Woodhill, Stoke St Gregory, Taunton, Somerset TA3 6EW (01823) 490296* **£50**; 6 rms, some with own bthrm and 2 in annexe. Very friendly 17th-c cottagey inn with a cosy and pleasantly romanticised stable theme, generous helpings of particularly good value food in no smoking dining room, excellent breakfasts, a decent wine list, and efficient service from hard-working family in charge; seats out on enclosed terrace; self-catering nearby; partial disabled access; dogs welcome in bedrooms

TAUNTON Castle *Castle Green, Taunton, Somerset TA1 1NF (01823) 272671* **£180***, plus special breaks; 44 lovely rms. Appealingly modernised partly Norman castle, its front almost smothered in wisteria, with fine old oak furniture, tapestries and paintings in comfortably elegant lounges, really excellent modern English cooking, good breakfasts, a range of good value wines from a thoughtful list, and efficient friendly service; pretty garden; disabled access; dogs welcome in bedrooms

WELLS Infield House *36 Portway, Wells, Somerset BA5 2BN (01749) 670989* **£49**, plus winter breaks; 3 comfortable rms (best view from back one). Carefully restored no smoking Victorian town house with period furnishings and family portraits, elegant lounge (with lots of local guidebooks), good breakfasts in dining room with Adam-style fireplace, evening meals by arrangement, and friendly personal service; cl 1 wk early Dec, 1 wk Jan; children over 12; dogs welcome in bedrooms

WOOKEY HOLE Glencot House *Glencot Lane, Wookey Hole, Wells, Somerset BA5 1BH (01749) 677160* **£88**; 13 rms, many with four-posters. In 18 acres of gardens and parkland (with own cricket pitch), this Jacobean-style Victorian mansion has some fine panelling, carved ceilings, antiques and flowers in the public rooms and hallways, a friendly atmosphere, and good food in the restaurant; fishing, table tennis, snooker, and small indoor jet stream pool; two friendly dogs and pet pig, lots to do nearby; cl 31 Dec for several days; they are kind to children; dogs welcome in bedrooms

Dog Friendly Pubs

CROWCOMBE

Carew Arms *Village (and pub) signposted just off A358 Taunton–Minehead*
17th-c beamed village inn quite untouched by modern fads: long benches, scrubbed tables, dark flagstones and hunting trophies, with well kept real ales and strong farm cider, lively local chat, good hearty food using local produce and game, picnic-sets out behind; a good value place to stay, in a quiet spot below the Quantocks
Free house ~ Licensees Simon Jones and Sheila Hartley-Dobbs ~ Real ale ~ Bar food (not Sun evening or Mon (except bank hols)) ~ Restaurant ~ No credit cards ~ (01984) 618631 ~ Children in lounge, restaurant and skittle alley ~ Dogs welcome ~ Annual folk festival during last weekend in Sept ~ Open 11.30–3.30,

6–11; 12–3.30, 7–10.30 Sun; closed winter Sun evening ~ Bedrooms: £22/£44

PORTISHEAD

Windmill *3¾ miles from M5 junction 17; A369 into town, then follow 'Sea Front' sign off left and into Nore Road*

Three-level all-day family dining pub with efficient central ordering system for good value generous food, good real ales, great view over the Bristol Channel to Newport and Cardiff, simple easy-going no smoking family area, tables out on terrace; pleasant coastal walks here

Free house ~ Licensee J S Churchill ~ Real ale ~ Bar food (12–9.30 all week) ~ (01275) 843677 ~ Children in family area ~ Dogs allowed in bar ~ Open 11–11; 12–10.30 Sun

STOGUMBER

White Horse *From A358 Taunton–Williton, village signposted on left at Crowcombe*

Long neat bar with warm winter fires and interesting village photographs, decent straightforward bar food at low prices, tables in quiet garden

Free house ~ Licensees Graham Roy and Edith Boada ~ Real ale ~ Bar food ~ (01984) 656277 ~ Children in eating area of bar and restaurant ~ Dogs welcome ~ Open 11.30–2.30, 6.30–11; 12–3, 7–10.30 Sun ~ Bedrooms: I£40B

TRISCOMBE

Blue Ball *Village signposted off A358 Crowcombe–Bagborough; turn off opposite sign to youth hostel; OS Sheet 181, map reference 155355*

Three-level bar in 15th-c thatched former coaching stables, fantastic choice of wines, very good inventive food, friendly helpful staff; two tortoisehell cats, whippets, and a lurcher; the decking at the top of the woodside terraced garden makes the most of the Quantock views

Free house ~ Licensee Patrick Groves ~ Real ale ~ Bar food (12–1.45, 7–9) ~ Restaurant ~ No credit cards ~ (01984) 618242 ~ Well behaved children welcome ~ Dogs welcome ~ Open 12–2.30, 7–11; 12–3, 7–10.30 Sun

STAFFORDSHIRE

Dog Friendly Hotels and B&Bs

BETLEY Adderley Green Farm *Heighley Castle Lane, Betley, Crewe, Cheshire CW3 9BA* (01270) 820203 **£45***; 3 rms. Georgian farmhouse on big dairy farm, with good breakfasts in homely dining room, and large garden; cl Christmas and New Year; children over 5; dogs allowed by prior arrangement

HOPWAS Oak Tree Farm *Hints Rd, Hopwas, Tamworth, Staffordshire B78 3AA* (01827) 56807 **£75**; 8 comfortable, spacious and pretty rms. Carefully restored no smoking farmhouse with elegant little lounge, fresh flowers, an attractive breakfast room, a friendly atmosphere, enjoyable breakfasts, gardens overlooking the River Tame, and an indoor swimming pool and steam room; cl Christmas–New Year; no children; disabled access; dogs welcome in bedrooms

OAKAMOOR Bank House *Farley Lane, Oakamoor, Stoke-on-Trent, Staffordshire ST10 3BD* (01538) 702810 **£80**, plus special breaks; 3 lovely big rms. Carefully restored no smoking country home in neat gardens on the edge of the Peak National Park, with lovely views; log fire in comfortable drawing room, library, piano in the inner hall, and most enjoyable food (by prior arrangement using home-grown and local produce) – super home-made breads, brioches, pastries and jams and marmalade at marvellous breakfast; friendly dog and cats; lots to do nearby; cl Christmas wk; dogs welcome by prior arrangement only

ROLLESTON ON DOVE Brookhouse Hotel *Station Rd, Rolleston on Dove, Burton upon Trent, Staffordshire DE13 9AA (01283) 814188* **£105***, plus wknd breaks; 19 comfortable rms with Victorian brass or four-poster beds. Handsome ivy-covered William & Mary brick building in five acres of lovely gardens with comfortable antiques-filled rooms, and good food using seasonal local produce in elegant little dining room; children over 12; disabled access; dogs welcome in bedrooms

SUFFOLK

Dog Friendly Hotels and B&Bs

BILDESTON Crown *High St, Bildeston, Ipswich, Suffolk IP7 7EB (01449) 740510* **£65**, plus special breaks; 13 individually furnished rms. Lovely timber-framed Tudor inn with a comfortable well furnished beamed lounge (refurbished under the new licensees), open fires, good food in popular restaurant, welcoming courteous service, an attractive two-acre informal garden – and resident ghost; self-catering apartment; disabled access; dogs welcome

BURY ST EDMUNDS Angel *3 Angel Hill, Bury St Edmunds, Suffolk IP33 1LT (01284) 753926* **£113**, plus special breaks; 65 individually decorated rms. Thriving creeper- clad 15th-c country-town hotel with particularly friendly staff, comfortable lounge and relaxed bar, log fires and fresh flowers, and good food in elegant restaurant and downstairs medieval vaulted room (Mr Pickwick enjoyed a roast dinner here); disabled access; dogs welcome in bedrooms

CAMPSEY ASH Old Rectory *Station Rd, Campsey Ash, Woodbridge, Suffolk IP13 0PU (01728) 746524* **£65**, plus special breaks; 7 comfortable, pretty rms. Very relaxed and welcoming no smoking Georgian house by church, with charming owner and staff, log fire in comfortable and restful drawing room, quite a few Victorian prints, first class food from a set menu in summer conservatory or two other dining rooms with more log fires, a good honesty bar, a sensational wine list with very modest mark-ups on its finest wines, and sizeable homely gardens; cl Christmas, 3 wks Feb–Mar; dogs welcome in bedrooms

HADLEIGH Edgehall *2 High St, Hadleigh, Ipswich, Suffolk IP7 5AP (01473) 822458* **£65***, plus special breaks; 8 pretty rms. Friendly family-run Tudor house with Georgian façade, comfortable carefully restored rooms, personal service, traditional English cooking using home-grown produce in no smoking dining room, and attractive walled garden with croquet; self-catering also; dogs welcome in bedrooms

HARTEST Hatch *Cross Green, Hartest, Bury St Edmunds, Suffolk IP29 4ED (01284) 830226* **£60**; 2 comfortable, pretty rms. Charming 15th-c thatched cottage with warmly welcoming owners, a lovely beamed drawing room with antiques, separate dining room for enjoyable breakfasts, afternoon tea, log fires, conservatory, seats out on terrace, and peaceful garden; occasional evening meals, and the nearby Crown does enjoyable food; no smoking; cl Christmas; children over 9 (though babies welcome);

limited disabled access; dogs welcome in bedrooms

HIGHAM Old Vicarage *Higham Rd, Higham, Colchester, Essex CO7 6JY (01206) 337248* **£58**, plus special breaks; 3 rms, 2 with own bthrm. Charming Tudor house nr quiet village with very friendly owners, pretty sitting room with fresh flowers, log fire and antiques, and enjoyable breakfasts in attractive breakfast room; play room with toys for children, grounds and fine gardens with river views (they have boats), tennis court, trampoline, and heated swimming pool; dogs welcome

HINTLESHAM Hintlesham Hall *Hintlesham, Ipswich, Suffolk IP8 3NS (01473) 652334* **£110***, plus special breaks; 33 lovely rms. Magnificent mansion, mainly Georgian but dating from Elizabethan times, in 175 acres with big walled gardens, 18-hole golf course, outdoor heated swimming pool, croquet, and tennis; restful and comfortable day rooms with books, antiques and open fires, fine modern cooking in several restaurants, a marvellous wine list, and exemplary service; snooker, sauna, steam room, gym, and beauty salon; well behaved children over 10 in evening restaurant; dogs welcome in bedrooms

LAVENHAM Angel *Market Pl, Lavenham, Sudbury, Suffolk CO10 9QZ (01787) 247388* **£75***, plus special breaks; 8 comfortable rms. 15th-c inn with original cellar and pargeted ceiling in attractive residents' lounge, several Tudor features such as a rare shuttered shop window front, civilised atmosphere, good food in bar and restaurant (they smoke their own meat and fish), lots of decent wines, several malt whiskies, well kept real ales, thoughtful friendly service, and maybe live classical piano Fri pm; cl 25–26 Dec; disabled access; dogs welcome in bedrooms

LAVENHAM Swan *High St, Lavenham, Sudbury, Suffolk*

CO10 9QA (01787) 247477 **£140**; 51 smart rms. Handsome and comfortable Elizabethan hotel that incorporates several fine half-timbered buildings inc an Elizabethan house and the former wool hall; lots of cosy seating areas, interesting historic prints and alcoves with beams, timbers, armchairs and settees, good food in lavishly timbered no smoking restaurant with a minstrels' gallery (actually built only in 1965), afternoon teas, intriguing little bar, and friendly helpful staff; disabled access; dogs welcome

LONG MELFORD Bull *Hall St, Long Melford, Sudbury, Suffolk CO10 9JG (01787) 378494* **£120***, plus special breaks; 25 rms, ancient or comfortably modern. An inn since 1580, this fine black and white hotel was originally a medieval manorial hall, and has handsome and interesting carved woodwork and timbering, and an old weavers' gallery overlooking the courtyard; a large log fire, old-fashioned and antique furnishings, enjoyable food, and friendly service; dogs by prior arrangement

ROUGHAM Ravenwood Hall *Rougham, Bury St Edmunds, Suffolk IP30 9JA (01359) 270345* **£96***, plus special breaks; 14 comfortable rms with antiques, some rms in mews. Tranquil Tudor country house in seven acres of carefully tended gardens and woodland; log fire in comfortable lounge, cosy bar, good food in timbered restaurant with big inglenook fireplace (home-preserved fruits and veg, home-smoked meats and fish), a good wine list, and helpful service; croquet and heated swimming pool; they are kind to children and have themed occasions for them and lots of animals; disabled access; dogs welcome away from restaurant

WOODBRIDGE Seckford Hall *Seckford Hall Rd, Great Bealings, Woodbridge, Suffolk IP13 6NU (01394) 385678* **£120**, plus special breaks; 32 comfortable rms. Handsome

Tudor mansion in 34 acres of gardens and parkland with carp-filled lake, putting, and leisure club with indoor heated pool, beauty salon, and gym in lovely tithe barn; fine linenfold panelling, huge fireplaces, heavy beams, plush furnishings and antiques in comfortable day rooms, good food (inc lovely teas with home-made cakes), and helpful service; cl 25 Dec; dogs welcome in bedrooms

WORLINGTON Worlington Hall *Mildenhall Rd, Worlington, Bury St Edmunds, Suffolk IP28 8RX (01638) 712237 £75*, plus special breaks; 9 comfortable rms with decanter of sherry and fruit. 16th-c former manor house in five acres with a 9-hole pitch and putt course, comfortable panelled lounge bar with log fire, good food in relaxed candlelit bistro, and friendly staff; dogs welcome

Dog Friendly Pubs

CHELMONDISTON

Butt & Oyster *Pin Mill – signposted from B1456 SE of Ipswich*
Bay windows overlooking River Orwell, with moored sailing barges and ships coming down from Ipswich; timeless well worn smoke room with model sailing ships, beady-eyed fish and high-backed settles, good value straightforward bar food
Pubmaster ~ Tenant Steve Lomas ~ Real ale ~ Restaurant ~ (01473) 780764 ~ Children in restaurant ~ Dogs allowed in bar ~ Open 11–11; 12–10.30 Sun

DUNWICH

Ship *St James Street*
Cosy nautical main bar with pews, tiles and woodburner,

friendly helpful staff, good bustling atmosphere, popular no-nonsense food inc fish bought straight from boats on the beach, no smoking restaurant; plenty of pleasant garden tables, good bedrooms, fine surrounding walks

Free house ~ Licensee David Sheldrake ~ Real ale ~ Bar food (12–7, 7–9) ~ (01728) 648219 ~ Children in restaurant and family room ~ Dogs allowed in bar and bedrooms ~ Open 11–11; 12–10.30 Sun; cl 3–6 in winter ~ Bedrooms: £50S/£60S

SOUTHWOLD

Harbour Inn *Blackshore, by the boats; from A1095, turn right at the Kings Head, and keep on past the golf course and water tower*

Interesting old waterside place among the small black fishing huts, with lifeboatman landlord and genuine nautical character: tiles, low beams and stripped panelling, lots of nauticalia, good value food inc fish and chips, plenty of tables outside by the jumbly waterfront bustle

Adnams ~ Tenant Colin Fraser ~ Real ale ~ Bar food (12–2.30, 6–9) ~ (01502) 722381 ~ Children welcome away from bar ~ Dogs allowed in bar ~ Live rock, folk Fri, Sat ~ Open 11–11; 12–10.30 Sun

WALBERSWICK

Bell *Just off B1387*

Unpretentious old pub in lovely setting close to the beach, tables on sizeable lawn, rambling traditional bar with well worn flagstones, ancient beams and high-backed settles, generous food, two resident boxer dogs

Adnams ~ Tenant Sue Ireland Cutting ~ Real ale ~ Bar food ~ Restaurant ~ No credit cards ~ (01502) 723109 ~ Children in family room ~ Dogs allowed in bar and bedrooms ~ Open 11–3, 6–11(all day during school hols); 11–11 Sat; 12–10.30 Sun ~ Bedrooms: £60S/£70S(£90B)

WALDRINGFIELD
Maybush *Off A12 S of Martlesham; The Quay, Cliff Road*
Busy family pub in beautiful spot with lots of tables out by the bird-haunted River Deben, big nautical bar, prompt friendly service, decent food with some emphasis on fish; plenty of the locals bring their dogs
Pubmaster ~ Tenants Steve and Louise Lomas ~ Real ale ~ Bar food (12–2.30, 6.30–9.30; 12–9.30 Sat, Sun) ~ Restaurant ~ (01473) 736215 ~ Children in restaurant ~ Dogs allowed in bar ~ Open 11–11; 12–10.30 Sun

WESTLETON
Crown *B1125 Blythburgh–Leiston*
Extended coaching inn with enjoyable bar lunches and appealing parlour bar with big log fire and nice mix of old settles and other furnishings, good beers, wines and malt whiskies, more ambitious restaurant menu; charming garden with pets corner and stables still used by horses
Free house ~ Licensees Richard and Rosemary Price ~ Real ale ~ Bar food (12–2.15, 7–9.30) ~ Restaurant ~ (01728) 648777 ~ Dogs allowed in bar and bedrooms ~ Open 11–3, 6–11; 12–3, 7–10.30 Sun; closed 25 and 26 Dec ~ Bedrooms: £59.50B/£74.50B

SURREY

Dog Friendly Hotels and B&Bs

BAGSHOT Pennyhill Park *College Ride, Bagshot, Surrey GU19 5ET (01276) 471774* **£228**, plus special breaks; 123 individually designed luxury rms and suites. Impressive

Victorian country house in 120 acres of well kept gardens and parkland inc a 9-hole golf course, tennis courts, outdoor heated swimming pool, clay pigeon shooting, archery, fishing, and an international rugby pitch; friendly courteous staff, wood-panelled bar with resident pianist, comfortable two-level lounge and reading room, very good imaginative food in two restaurants, jazz Sun lunchtime, and terraces overlooking the golf course; disabled access; dogs welcome in bedrooms

CHERTSEY Crown 7 London St, Chertsey, Surrey KT16 8AP (01932) 564657 **£65**w; 30 comfortable modern rms. Bustling, friendly place with some original features and open fire in large bar, conservatory extension, good food, attractive restaurant, and lovely big garden; disabled access; dogs welcome

HASLEMERE Deerfell Blackdown, Haslemere, Surrey GU27 3LA (01428) 653409 **£48***; 3 comfortable rms. Comfortable no smoking stone coach house with wonderful views and good nearby walks; generous meals in handsome dining room (ordered in advance), open fire in sitting room, pictures, antiques and old rugs, a sun room, good breakfasts, and friendly owners; cl mid-Dec to mid-Jan; children over 6; dogs by prior arrangement

HASLEMERE Lythe Hill Hotel & Spa Petworth Rd, Haslemere, Surrey GU27 3BQ (01428) 651251 **£153**, plus special breaks; 41 individually styled rms, a few in the original house. Lovely partly 15th-c building in 20 acres of parkland and bluebell woods (adjoining the NT hillside) with floodlit tennis court, croquet lawn, and jogging track; plush, comfortable and elegant lounges, a relaxed bar, two no smoking restaurants (one with French cooking, the other with traditional English), and good attentive service; new spa with swimming pool, sauna, steam and beauty rooms and gym; disabled access; dogs welcome in bedrooms

NUTFIELD Nutfield Priory *Nutfield, Redhill, Surrey RH1 4EL (01737) 822066* **£150**, plus special breaks; 60 rms. Impressive Victorian Gothic hotel in 40 acres of parkland with lovely elaborate carvings, stained-glass windows, gracious day rooms, a fine panelled library, cloistered restaurant, and even an organ in the galleried grand hall; extensive leisure club with indoor heated swimming pool; dogs welcome in bedrooms

Dog Friendly Pubs

REIGATE HEATH
Skimmington Castle *3 miles from M25 junction 8: through Reigate take A25 towards Dorking, then on edge of Reigate turn left past Black Horse into Flanchford Road; after ½ mile turn left into Bonny's Road (unmade, very bumpy track); after crossing golf course fork right up hill*
Quaint old country pub handy for North Downs rambles, informal mix of furnishings including old-fashioned settles, dark panelling, beams and big brick fireplace, small no smoking back family room (children do need to behave here), good popular bar food and drinks choice, prompt friendly service; nice views from tables outside, hitching rail for horses
Pubmaster ~ Tenants Anthony Pugh and John Davidson ~ Real ale ~ Bar food (12–2.15(2.30 Sun), 7–9) ~ (01737) 243100 ~ Dogs welcome ~ Folk second Sun of month ~ Open 11–3, 5.30(6 Sat)–11; 12–10.30 Sun; closed evenings 25–27 Dec and 1 Jan

SUSSEX

Dog Friendly Hotels and B&Bs

ALFRISTON George *High St, Alfriston, Polegate, East Sussex BN26 5SY (01323) 870319* **£60**; 7 rms. 14th-c timbered inn opposite the intriguing façade of the Red Lion, with massive low beams hung with hops, appropriately soft lighting, a log fire (or summer flower arrangement) in a huge stone inglenook, lots of copper and brass, plenty of sturdy stripped tables, and a thriving atmosphere; popular home-made food, a cosy candlelit restaurant, nice breakfasts, well kept real ales, and a jovial landlord; seats out in the charming flint-walled garden behind; dogs welcome in bedrooms

BATTLE Little Hemingfold Hotel *189 Hastings Rd, Battle, East Sussex TN33 0TT (01424) 774338* **£88***, plus special breaks; 12 rms. Partly 17th-c, partly early Victorian farmhouse in 40 acres of woodland, with trout lake, tennis, gardens, and lots of walks (the two Labradors may come with you); comfortable sitting rooms, open fires, restful atmosphere and very good food using home-grown produce at own candlelit table; tennis court; children over 7; cl 2 Jan–13 Feb; dogs welcome in bedrooms

BATTLE Powder Mills *Powdermill Lane, Battle, East Sussex TN33 0SP (01424) 775511* **£105**, plus special breaks; 40 rms, some in annexe. Attractive 18th-c creeper-clad manor house in 150 acres of park and woodland with four lakes and outdoor swimming pool, and next to the 1066 Battle-field; country-house atmosphere, log fires and antiques in elegant day rooms, attentive service, and good modern cooking in Orangery restaurant; children over 10 in evening restaurant; well behaved dogs by prior arrangement; disabled access; dogs welcome

BOSHAM Millstream *Bosham Lane, Bosham, Chichester, West Sussex PO18 8HL (01243) 573234* **£130**; 35 rms. Warmly friendly hotel in charming waterside village, with attractive bar and sitting room, open fire and fresh flowers, very good food using fresh local produce, good wine list, streamside garden; disabled access; dogs welcome in bedrooms

BRIGHTON Grand *97–99 Kings Rd, Brighton, East Sussex BN1 2FW (01273) 321188* **£230**, plus special breaks; 200 handsome rms, many with sea view. Famous Victorian hotel with marble columns and floors and fine moulded plasterwork in the luxurious and elegant day rooms; good service, very good food and fine wines, popular afternoon tea in sunny conservatory, a bustling nightclub, and health spa with indoor swimming pool; disabled access; dogs welcome in bedrooms

CHICHESTER Suffolk House *East Row, Chichester, West Sussex PO19 1PD (01243) 778899* **£95**, plus winter breaks; 11 rms, some overlooking garden. Friendly Georgian house in centre and close to the cathedral, with homely comfortable lounge, little bar, traditional cooking in no smoking restaurant, good breakfasts, and small walled garden; disabled access; dogs by arrangement

CLIMPING Bailiffscourt *Climping St, Climping, Littlehampton, East Sussex BN17 5RW (01903) 723511* **£160**, plus special breaks; 32 rms, many with four-poster beds and winter log fires, and with super views. Mock 13th-c manor built only 60 years ago but with tremendous character – fine old iron-studded doors, huge fireplaces, heavy beams and so forth –

in 30 acres of coastal pastures and walled gardens: elegant furnishings, enjoyable modern English and French food, fine wines, a relaxed atmosphere, and outdoor swimming pool, tennis and croquet; children over 7 in restaurant; disabled access; dogs welcome away from restaurant

FAIRLIGHT Fairlight Cottage *Warren Rd, Fairlight, Hastings, East Sussex TN35 4AG (01424) 812545* **£50**, plus winter breaks; 3 rms, one with four-poster. Comfortable and very friendly no smoking house in fine countryside with views over Rye Bay and plenty of rural and clifftop walks; big comfortable lounge (nice views), good breakfasts in elegant dining room or on new balcony, and generous carefully prepared food (by prior arrangement, but not at Christmas); children over 7; dogs welcome

FRANT Old Parsonage *Church Lane, Frant, Tunbridge Wells, Kent TN3 9DX (01892) 750773* **£84***, plus special breaks; 4 very pretty rms, 2 with four-posters. Just two miles from Tunbridge Wells, this carefully restored imposing former Georgian rectory has antiques, watercolours and plants in elegant sitting rooms, a spacious Victorian conservatory, good food in candlelit dining room, and balustraded terrace overlooking quiet 3-acre garden; several nearby walks; children over 7; dogs welcome in bedrooms

PEASMARSH Flackley Ash *Peasmarsh, Rye, East Sussex TN31 6YH (01797) 230651* **£124**; 45 rooms. Attractive and extended Georgian house in 5 acres of landscaped gardens with croquet and putting; good, nicely presented food using local produce in the conservatory or dining room, log fire in lounge bar, and indoor heated pool and leisure centre; dogs welcome in bedrooms

RUSHLAKE GREEN Stone House *Rushlake Green, Heathfield, East Sussex TN21 9QJ (01435) 830553* **£145**; 7

rms, some with four-posters. In a thousand acres of pretty countryside (with plenty of walks and country sports) and surrounded by an 18th-c walled garden, this lovely house was built at the end of the 15th c and extended in Georgian times; there are open log fires, antiques and family heirlooms in the drawing room, a quiet library, an antique full-sized table in the mahogany-panelled billiard room, wonderful food in the panelled dining room, fine breakfasts, and a cosseting atmosphere; cl 24 Dec–1 Jan; children over 9; dogs welcome in bedrooms

RYE Jeakes House *Mermaid St, Rye, East Sussex TN31 7ET (01797) 222828* **£84**; 12 rms overlooking the rooftops of this medieval town or across the marsh to the sea, 10 with own bthrm. Fine 16th-c building, well run and friendly, with good breakfasts, lots of well worn books, comfortable furnishings, linen and lace, a warm fire, and lovely peaceful atmosphere; children over 11; dogs welcome in bedrooms

SHIPLEY Goffsland Farm *Shipley Rd, Southwater, Horsham, West Sussex RH13 7BQ (01403) 730434* **£44**; 2 rms, 1 family rm with own sitting/dining rm and own access. 17th-c Wealden farmhouse on 260-acre family farm with good breakfasts, afternoon tea and evening meals by arrangement, and a friendly welcome; horse riding and plenty of surrounding walks; dogs welcome

TILLINGTON Horse Guards *Tillington, Petworth, West Sussex GU28 9AF (01798) 342332* **£75**; 3 spacious clean rms. Pretty 18th-c dining pub in lovely village setting with neatly kept and cosy beamed front bar, imaginative restaurant-style food, 10 wines by the glass, and real ales; children must be over 7 in evening restaurant; dogs allowed if well behaved

Dog Friendly Pubs

BILLINGSHURST
Blue Ship *The Haven; hamlet signposted off A29 just N of junction with A264, then follow signpost left towards Garlands and Okehurst*

Genuinely unspoilt and peaceful country pub with beams, scrubbed tables on brick floor, good beer from the hatch, inglenook log fire, reasonably priced traditional bar food; a lovely spot in summer, with a play area

Badger ~ Tenant J R Davie ~ Real ale ~ Bar food (not Sun or Mon evenings) ~ No credit cards ~ (01403) 822709 ~ Children in two rooms without bar ~ Dogs welcome ~ Open 11–3, 6–11; 12–3.30, 7–10.30 Sun

CHARLTON
Fox Goes Free *Village signposted off A286 Chichester–Midhurst in Singleton, also from Chichester–Petworth via East Dean*

Cheerful old pub below the South Downs with dark and cosy series of separate rooms, standing timbers, beams and log fires, good, interesting bar food, attractive secluded garden with several terraces and notable downland view; the friendly Jack Russell is called Wiggles and the black cat, Guinness

Free house ~ Licensee Oliver Ligertwood ~ Real ale ~ Bar food (12–2.30(3 Sat and Sun), 6.15(6 Sat and Sun)–10.30(10 Sun)) ~ Restaurant ~ (01243) 811461 ~ Children in eating area of bar and restaurant ~ Dogs allowed in bar and bedrooms ~ Live music Weds evening ~ Open 11–3, 5.30–11; 11–11 Sat; 12–10.30 Sun; 11–4, 5.30–11 Sat, 12–4, 6–10.30 Sun in winter; closed evening 25 Dec ~ Bedrooms: £40S/£60S

EAST DEAN
Tiger *Pub (with village centre) signposted – not vividly – from A259 Eastbourne–Seaford*

Traditional pub on delightful cottage-lined green, two smallish rooms (candlelit at night) with low beams, antique settles, old prints and pewter, good food very strong on local produce (great choice of lunchtime ploughman's); on South Downs Way, and the lane leads on down to a fine stretch of coast culminating in Beachy Head; no children inside

Free house ~ Licensee Nicholas Denyer ~ Real ale ~ Bar food ~ No credit cards ~ (01323) 423209 ~ Dogs welcome ~ Morris dancers on bank hols, mummers 26 Dec ~ Open 11–3, 6–11; 11–11 Sat; 12–10.30 Sun

HEATHFIELD
Star *Old Heathfield – head East out of Heathfield itself on A265, then fork right on to B2096; turn right at signpost to Heathfield Church then keep bearing right; pub on left immediately after church*

14th-c pilgrims' inn with relaxed and chatty L-shaped beamed and panelled candlelit bar, fine inglenook log fire, decent blackboard choice of enjoyable bar food; prettily planted sloping garden with lovely views of rolling oak-lined sheep pastures

Free house ~ Licensees Mike Chappell and Fiona Airey ~ Real ale ~ Bar food (12–2.15(2.30 wknds), 7–9.30) ~ Restaurant ~ (01435) 863570 ~ Children in eating area of bar ~ Dogs welcome ~ Open 11.30–3, 5.30–11; 12–3, 7–10.30 Sun

HENLEY
Duke of Cumberland Arms *Village signposted just off A286 S of Fernhurst, N of Midhurst; if coming from Midhurst, take 1st turn into village, then keep bearing right; OS Sheet 186, map reference 894258*

Tucked-away two-room 15th-c cottage with low ceilings, log fires, gas lamps, scrubbed rough oak tables, and enjoyable food inc their own fresh trout; the bulldog is called Jasper, and the sloping pond-side garden is rather special, with lovely views over Black Down and the wooded hills
Free house ~ Licensees Gaston Duval and Christina Duval ~ Real ale ~ Bar food (12–3, 7–9.30; not Sun evening) ~ Restaurant ~ (01428) 652280 ~ Children welcome ~ Dogs welcome ~ Open 11–3, 5–11; 12–3, 7–10.30 Sun

WINEHAM

Royal Oak *Village signposted from A272 and B2116*
Lovely old-fashioned unchanging pub, very low beams, log fire in enormous inglenook, quiet country views from back parlour, beers tapped from the cask, food limited to sandwiches, ploughman's and winter soup, courteous service – in the same family for over 50 years; tables by well on attractive front lawn, no children inside
Inn Business ~ Tenant Tim Peacock ~ Real ale ~ Bar food (11–2.30, 5.30–10.30) ~ No credit cards ~ (01444) 881252 ~ Dogs welcome ~ Open 11–2.30, 5.30(6 Sat)–11; 12–3, 7–10.30 Sun

WARWICKSHIRE

Dog Friendly Hotels and B&Bs

BISHOP'S TACHBROOK Mallory Court *Harbury Lane, Bishop's Tachbrook, Leamington Spa, Warwickshire CV33 9QB (01926) 330214* **£195***, plus special breaks; 18 wonderfully comfortable and luxurious rms. Fine ancient-looking house – actually built around 1910 – with elegant antiques and flower-filled day rooms, attentive staff, and excellent food using home-grown produce in oak panelled restaurant; ten acres of lovely gardens with outdoor swimming pool, tennis, and croquet; children over 9; dogs welcome in bedrooms

BLACKWELL Blackwell Grange *Blackwell, Shipston-on-Stour, Warwickshire CV36 4PF (01608) 682357* **£60***; 3 pretty rms. 17th-c Cotswold farmhouse with log fire in comfortable beamed sitting room, large inglenook fireplace in flagstoned dining room, good home cooking using own free-range eggs (evening meal by arrangement; bring your own wine), pretty garden, and nice country views; cl 24–25 Dec; children over 12, but parents with younger children stay in annexe; good disabled access; dogs by arrangement

HOCKLEY HEATH Nuthurst Grange *Nuthurst Grange Road, Hockley Heath, Solihull, West Midlands B94 5NL (01564) 783972* **£155***, plus special breaks; 15 comfortable, spacious rms with lots of extras. Red brick, creeper-clad Edwardian house in landscaped gardens, with light, airy and prettily decorated public rooms, lovely fresh flowers, enjoyable modern British cooking using home-grown produce, good breakfasts, and pleasant helpful staff; cl 1 wk at Christmas; well behaved children welcome; disabled access; dogs welcome in bedrooms

LOXLEY Loxley Farm *Stratford Rd, Loxley, Warwick, Warwickshire CV35 9JN (01789) 840265* **£64***; 2 suites with their own sitting rooms in attractive barn conversion. Not far from Stratford, this tucked-away, thatched and half-timbered partly 14th-c house has low beams, wonky walls and floors, antiques and dried flowers, open fire, helpful friendly owners, and good Aga-cooked breakfasts; peaceful garden, and fine old village church; cl Christmas and New Year; dogs welcome in bedrooms

STRATFORD-UPON-AVON Caterham House *58–59 Rother St, Stratford-upon-Avon, Warwicks CV37 6LT* (01789) 267309 **£85**, 10 individually decorated rms with antiques and fresh flowers. Popular Georgian house just ten mins from Royal Shakespeare Theatre, and run for nearly 20 years by charming helpful owners; interestingly furnished sitting room opening on to pretty terrace, French country-style furniture, and excellent breakfasts (plenty of restaurants nearby for evening meals); cl Christmas; self-catering flat and cottage also; dogs welcome in bedrooms

STRATFORD-UPON-AVON Melita *37 Shipston Rd, Stratford-upon-Avon, Warwickshire CV37 7LN* (01789) 292432 **£69***, plus special breaks; 12 well equipped, no smoking rms. Friendly family-run Victorian hotel with pretty, carefully laid-out garden, comfortable lounge with open fire, extensive breakfasts; close to town centre and theatre; cl Christmas and New Year; dogs welcome in bedrooms

STRATFORD-UPON-AVON Shakespeare *Chapel St, Stratford-upon-Avon, Warwickshire CV37 6ER* (0870) 400 8182 **£151**, plus wknd breaks; 74 comfortable well equipped rms. Smart hotel based on handsome lavishly modernised Tudor merchants' houses, with comfortable bar, good food, quick friendly service, and civilised tea or coffee in peaceful chintzy armchairs by blazing log fires; seats out in back courtyard; three mins' walk from theatre; disabled access; dogs welcome in bedrooms

SUTTON COLDFIELD New Hall *New Hall Drive, Sutton Coldfield, West Midlands B76 1QX* (0121) 378 2442 **£153**w, plus special breaks; 60 lovely rms (the ones in the manor house are the best). England's oldest moated manor house, in 26 beautiful acres, with luxurious day rooms, a graceful panelled restaurant with carefully cooked imaginative food using the freshest (often home-grown) produce, and excellent service; they can hold wedding ceremonies, and have a leisure club; children over 8; disabled access; dogs welcome in bedrooms

Dog Friendly Pubs

ALDERMINSTER
Bell *A3400 Oxford–Stratford*
Imaginative food in civilised dining pub's spacious linked bar rooms, good range of wines by the glass, conservatory and terrace overlooking Stour Valley; readers with children have felt particularly welcome
Free house ~ Licensees Keith and Vanessa Brewer ~ Real ale ~ Bar food ~ Restaurant ~ (01789) 450414 ~ Children welcome ~ Dogs allowed in bar and bedrooms ~ Open 12–2.30, 7–11(10.30 Sun); closed evenings 23–30 Dec ~ Bedrooms: £25(£35S)/£45(£45S)(£62B)

LAPWORTH
Navigation *Old Warwick Road S of village (B4439 Warwick–Hockley Heath); by Grand Union Canal, OS Sheet 139, map reference 19170*
Bustling rustic local in pretty canalside setting, inglenook fire, canal memorabilia and high-backed settles in flagstoned bar, nicely done extension, cheery efficient landlord and staff, remarkably generous food, good real ales, farm cider and lots of malt whiskies; summer hatch service to waterside terrace
Voyager ~ Lease Andrew Kimber ~ Real ale ~ Bar food (12–2(3

Sun), 6–9) ~ (01564) 783337 ~ Children welcome ~ Dogs allowed in bar ~ Open 11–3, 5.30–11; 11–11 Sat; 12–10.30 Sun

WILTSHIRE

Dog Friendly Hotels and B&Bs

BRADFORD-ON-AVON Woolley Grange *Woolley Green, Bradford-on-Avon, Wiltshire BA15 1TX (01225) 864705* **£165**, plus winter breaks; 23 rms, with fruit and home-made biscuits. Civilised Jacobean manor house with a relaxed informal atmosphere, lovely flowers, log fires and antiques in comfortable and beautifully decorated day rooms, and pretty conservatory; delicious food using local (or home-grown) produce, often organic, inc home-baked breads and muffins and home-made jams and marmalades for breakfast, marvellous staff, and swimming pool, tennis, badminton, and croquet; particularly well organised for families, with nannies and plenty of entertainment; disabled access; dogs welcome in bedrooms

CHICKSGROVE Compasses *Lower Chicksgrove, Tisbury, Salisbury, Wiltshire SP3 6NB (01722) 714318* **£55**; 4 rms with showers. Lovely thatched house in delightful hamlet with old bottles and jugs hanging from the beams, good home-made food, well kept real ales, and peaceful farm courtyard and garden; dogs welcome in bedrooms

DEVIZES Bear *Market Pl, Devizes, Wiltshire SN10 1HS (01380) 722444* **£75***, plus special breaks; 24 rms. Very much at the town's heart, this 16th-c inn has an old-fashioned feel, a wide choice of food from snacks to more elaborate meals in the oak-panelled Lawrence Room, two more formal restaurants, beams, and fresh flowers; cl 25–26 Dec; dogs welcome in bedrooms

EBBESBOURNE WAKE Horseshoe *Ebbesbourne Wake, Salisbury, Wiltshire SP5 5JG (01722) 780474* **£60***; 2 rms. Particularly welcoming pub with beautifully kept little bar, open fire, fresh flowers and interesting bric-a-brac on beams, popular home-made food in bar or no smoking restaurant, big breakfasts and nice Sunday lunches, well kept real ales, pretty little garden, play area, and pets' corner in paddock; no children; cl 25 Dec; dogs welcome anywhere

HEYTESBURY Angel *High St, Heytesbury, Warminster, Wiltshire BA12 0ED (01985) 840330* **£65***; 8 comfortable rms. 16th-c coaching inn with armchairs, sofas, and a good fire in cosy homely lounge, a long beamed bar with woodburner, quite a few prints, and good service from friendly staff; well kept real ales, decent wines, and a wide choice of consistently good food in charming back dining room that opens on to secluded garden; dogs welcome in bedrooms

LACOCK At the Sign of the Angel *Church St, Lacock, Chippenham, Wiltshire SN15 2LB (01249) 730230* **£99**; 10 charming rms. This fine 15th-c house in a lovely NT village is full of character, with heavy oak furniture, beams and big fireplaces, a restful oak-panelled lounge, and good English cooking in three candlelit restaurants; cl Christmas wk; disabled access; dogs welcome in bedrooms

MALMESBURY Old Bell *Abbey Row, Malmesbury, Wiltshire SN16 0BW (01666) 822344* **£130***, plus special breaks; 31 rms. With some claim to being one of England's oldest hotels and standing in the shadow of the Norman abbey, this fine wisteria-clad building has traditionally furnished rooms with

Edwardian pictures, an early 13th-c hooded stone fireplace, two good fires and plenty of comfortable sofas, magazines and newspapers; cheerful helpful service, very good food, and attractively old-fashioned garden; particularly well organised for families; disabled access to ground floor bedroom; dogs welcome in bedrooms

NETTLETON Fosse Farmhouse Hotel *Nettleton, Chippenham, Wiltshire SN14 7NJ (01249) 782286* **£120***, plus special breaks (inc some interesting craft wknds); 5 rms. 18th-c Cotswold stone house extensively restored with decorative French antique furniture and pretty English chintzes; morning coffee, lunch and cream teas served on the lawns or in very attractive dining room; antiques shop with dried flowers and decorative items in former dairy behind the house; dogs welcome in bedrooms

PURTON Pear Tree *Church End, Purton, Swindon, Wiltshire SN5 4ED (01793) 772100* **£110***; 17 very comfortable, pretty rms. Impeccably run former vicarage with elegant comfortable day rooms, fresh flowers, fine conservatory restaurant with good modern English cooking using home-grown herbs, helpful caring staff, and 7½ acres inc a traditional Victorian garden; cl 26–30 Dec; disabled access; dogs welcome in bedrooms

SALISBURY Rose & Crown *Harnham Rd, Harnham, Salisbury, Wiltshire SP2 8JQ (01722) 399955* **£100***; 28 rms in the original building or smart modern extension. It's almost worth a visit just for the view – well nigh identical to that in the most famous Constable painting of Salisbury Cathedral; elegantly restored inn with friendly beamed and timbered bar, log fire, good bar and restaurant food, and charming Avonside garden; disabled access; dogs welcome in bedrooms

WARMINSTER Bishopstrow House *Bishopstrow, Warminster, Wiltshire BA12 9HH (01985) 212312* **£199***, plus special breaks; 32 sumptuous rms, some with jacuzzi. Charming ivy-clad Georgian house in 27 acres with heated indoor and outdoor swimming pools, indoor and outdoor tennis courts, fitness centre and beauty treatment rooms, and own fishing on River Wylye; very relaxed friendly atmosphere, log fires, lovely fresh flowers, antiques and fine paintings in boldly decorated day rooms, and really impressive food; disabled access; dogs anywhere except restaurant

Dog Friendly Pubs

ALVEDISTON
Crown *Village signposted on left off A30 about 12 miles W of Salisbury*
Lovely 15th-c thatched inn in peaceful pretty spot, three charming low-beamed and partly panelled rooms, imaginative food, attractive garden on several levels with play area, comfortable bedrooms (one is over the bar)
Free house ~ Licensee Elizabeth Pate ~ Real ale ~ Bar food (not Sun evening) ~ Restaurant ~ No credit cards ~ (01722) 780335 ~ Children in eating area of bar and family room ~ Dogs allowed in bar and bedrooms ~ Open 12–3, 6–11; 12–3, 7–10.30 Sun ~ Bedrooms: £25S/£47.50S

BRADFORD-ON-AVON
Cross Guns *Avoncliff; pub is across footbridge from Avoncliff Station (road signposted Turleigh turning left off A363 heading uphill N from river in Bradford centre, and keep bearing left), and can also be reached down very steep and eventually unmade road signposted Avoncliff – keep straight on rather than turning*

left into village centre – from Westwood (which is signposted from B3109 and from A366, W of Trowbridge)

Marvellous spot with lots of tables out on terraced floodlit gardens overlooking River Avon, canal, bridges and aqueducts; stripped stone, low beams, inglenook log fire, emphasis on very generous food in bar and new upstairs restaurant, but great range of drinks too; walkers very welcome, but not their muddy boots

Free house ~ Licensees Jenny and Ken Roberts ~ Real ale ~ Bar food (12–10) ~ Restaurant ~ (01225) 862335/867613 ~ Children welcome ~ Dogs allowed in bar ~ Open 10–12; closed 25, 26 Dec evening ~ Bedrooms: £45B/£80B

CORTON

Dove *Village signposted from A36 at Upton Lovell, SE of Warminster; this back road on the right bank of the River Wylye is a quiet alternative to the busy A36 Warminster–Wilton*

Pretty and cottagey country pub, attractive mix of furnishings around central log fire and in dining areas off inc conservatory, good well presented food inc lunchtime snacks and more elaborate evening dishes, good wines by the glass, attentive friendly staff; tables on neat back lawn

Free house ~ Licensee William Harrison-Allan ~ Real ale ~ Bar food (12–2.30, 7–9.30) ~ Restaurant ~ (01985) 850109 ~ Children welcome ~ Dogs allowed in bar and bedrooms ~ Open 12–3(4 Sat), 6.30–11; 12–4, 7–11 Sun ~ Bedrooms: £49.50S/£75S

FONTHILL GIFFORD

Beckford Arms *Off B3089 W of Wilton at Fonthill Bishop*

On the edge of a fine parkland estate with a lake and sweeping vistas, with big, light and airy bar rooms, enjoyable food using local produce, friendly staff and good bedrooms

Free house ~ Licensees Karen and Eddie Costello ~ Real ale ~ Bar

food (12–2, 7–9(9.30 Fri, Sat)) ~ Restaurant ~ (01747) 870385 ~ Children welcome ~ Dogs allowed in bar and bedrooms ~ Open 12–11; 12–10.30 Sun ~ Bedrooms: £40S/£70B

LACOCK

Rising Sun *Bewley Common, Bowden Hill – out towards Sandy Lane, up hill past Abbey; OS Sheet 173, map reference 935679*
Terrific views from big two-level terrace, welcoming and cheerfully unpretentious knocked-through stone-floored bar with rustic décor and furnishings, open fires, good beers and farm cider, generous home-made food from good baguettes up (only roast on Sun)
Free house ~ Licensees Sue Sturdy and Roger Catte ~ Real ale ~ Bar food (12–2, 7–9(9.30 Fri, Sat); not Sun–Tues evening) ~ (01249) 730363 ~ Children in eating area of bar till 9pm ~ Dogs welcome ~ Live music every Weds and alternate Sun from 3pm ~ Open 12–3, 6–11; 12–10.30 Sun; closed 25, 26 Dec evening, 1 Jan

SEEND

Barge *Seend Cleeve; signposted off A361 Devizes–Trowbridge, between Seend village and signpost to Seend Head*
Picnic-sets out in the neatly kept waterside garden make an ideal spot for watching the bustle of boats on the Kennet & Avon Canal with its good towpath walks; big log fire and unusual barge-theme décor, good generous food, lots of malts and mulled wine in winter; cheery service, barbecues outside on summer Sundays
Wadworths ~ Tenant Christopher Moorley Long ~ Real ale ~ Bar food (12–2, 7–9.30(10 Fri, Sat)) ~ Restaurant ~ (01380) 828230 ~ Children welcome ~ Dogs allowed in bar ~ Open 11–3, 6–11; 12–10.30 (12–4, 7–10.30 winter) Sun

WOOTTON RIVERS

Royal Oak *Village signposted from A346 Marlborough–*

Salisbury, from A345 Marlborough–Pewsey, and B3087 E of Pewsey

Beamed and thatched 16th-c pub popular for extensive range of food from lunchtime sandwiches to elaborate main meals, comfortable timbered bar, friendly low-beamed L-shaped dining lounge, good drinks choice; tables out in front, quite near Kennet & Avon Canal footpath

Free house ~ Licensees John and Rosa Jones ~ Real ale ~ Bar food (12–2.30, 7–9.30) ~ Restaurant ~ (01672) 810322 ~ Children welcome ~ Dogs allowed in bar and bedrooms ~ Open 10–3, 6–12; 12–4.30, 6–11.30 Sun ~ Bedrooms: £22.50(£35S)/£45(£50S)

WYLYE

Bell *Just off A303/A36 junction; High Street*

Cosy 14th-c pub in peaceful village, fine downland walks nearby, civilised unhurried atmosphere, well prepared bar food using fresh ingredients, well kept real ales from far and wide, nicely placed tables outside; good bedrooms

Free house ~ Licensees Keith and Linda Bidwell ~ Real ale ~ Bar food (12–2, 6–9.30; 12–2.30, 7–9 Sun) ~ Restaurant ~ (01985) 248338 ~ Children in restaurant ~ Dogs allowed in bar and bedrooms ~ Open 11.30–2.30, 6–11; 12–3, 7–10.30 Sun ~ Bedrooms: £35B/£45S(£60B)

WORCESTERSHIRE

Dog Friendly Hotels and B&Bs

BROADWAY Broadway Hotel *The Green, Broadway, Worcestershire WR12 7AA (01386) 852401* **£118**, plus special breaks; 20 well kept rms. Lovely 15th-c building, once a monastic guest house, with galleried and timbered lounge, cosy beamed bar, attractively presented food served by attentive staff in airy comfortable restaurant, and seats outside on terrace; disabled access; dogs welcome in bedrooms

BROADWAY Lygon Arms *High St, Broadway, Worcestershire WR12 7DU* (01386) 852255 **£229**, plus special breaks; 69 lovely period rms (some more modern, too). Handsome hotel where Oliver Cromwell and King Charles I once stayed; interesting beamed rooms, oak panelling, antiques, log fires, fine traditional food in the Great Hall with minstrels' gallery and heraldic frieze, excellent service, and charming garden; health spa; children over 8 in evening restaurant; disabled access; dogs welcome in bedrooms

EVESHAM Evesham Hotel *Coopers Lane, Off Waterside, Evesham, Worcestershire WR11 1DA* (01386) 765566 **£108***, plus special breaks; 40 spacious rms with games and jigsaws. Comfortably modernised and cheerful family-run hotel with a warmly friendly, relaxed and jokey atmosphere, popular restaurant with very good food (esp lunchtime buffet), huge wine and spirits list, and sitting room with games and toys; indoor swimming pool surrounded by table tennis and table football, and grounds with croquet, trampoline, swings and putting; particularly well organised for families (but they do not get overrun by children); cl 25–26 Dec; partial disabled access; dogs welcome in bedrooms

HIMBLETON Phepson Farm *Phepson, Droitwich, Worcestershire WR9 7JZ* (01905) 391205 **£50***, plus winter breaks; 6 rms, 4 in renovated farm buildings. Relaxed and friendly 17th-c farmhouse on small sheep farm with a fishing lake; a comfortable guests' lounge, good breakfasts in separate dining room; self-catering apartment; cl Christmas and New Year; partial disabled access; dogs welcome in bedrooms

MALVERN Cowleigh Park Farm *Cowleigh Park, Cradley, Malvern, Worcestershire WR13 5HJ (01684) 566750* **£56***; 3 rms. Carefully restored and furnished black and white timbered 17th-c farmhouse in own grounds, surrounded by lovely countryside, with good breakfasts and light suppers or full evening meals (prior booking); self-catering also; cl Christmas; children over 7; dogs welcome in bedrooms

MALVERN WELLS Cottage in the Wood *Holywell Rd, Malvern, Worcestershire WR14 4LG (01684) 575859* **£95***, plus special breaks; 20 compact but pretty rms, some in separate nearby cottages. Family-run Georgian dower house with quite splendid views across the Severn Valley and marvellous walks from the grounds; antiques, log fires, comfortable seats and magazines in public rooms, and modern English cooking and an extensive wine list in attractive no smoking restaurant; dogs welcome in bedrooms

Dog Friendly Pubs

KIDDERMINSTER
King & Castle *Railway Station, Comberton Hill*
Re-creation of a classic station refreshment room beside Britain's most lively private steam railway, plenty of railway memorabilia, good real ales and bargain food
Free house ~ Licensee Rosemary Hyde ~ Real ale ~ Bar food (12–2(2.30 Sat, Sun), 6–8 Fri–Sun; not Mon–Thurs evenings) ~ No credit cards ~ (01562) 747505 ~ Children in eating area of bar ~ Dogs welcome ~ Open 11–3, 5–11; 11–11 Sat; 12–10.30 Sun

YORKSHIRE
NORTH YORK MOORS & EAST YORKSHIRE

Dog Friendly Hotels and B&Bs

BLAKEY RIDGE Lion *High Blakey, Kirkbymoorside, York YO62 7LQ* (01751) 417320 **£58***, plus winter breaks; 10 good rms, most with own bthrm. The fourth-highest inn in England, this has spectacular moorland views, rambling beamed stripped stone bars, blazing fires, generous helpings of decent food served all day, good breakfasts, candlelit restaurant, quite a few real ales, and genuinely friendly licensees and staff; monthly live music nights; fine walking country; disabled access; dogs welcome in bedrooms

EGTON BRIDGE Horse Shoe *Egton Bridge, Whitby, North Yorkshire YO21 1XE* (01947) 895245 **£50**, plus special breaks; 6 simple rms, most with own bthrm. Beautifully placed inn by River Esk (stepping stones big enough for children to sit on), with lots of friendly wild birds and a pleasant sheltered lawn; open fires, attractive traditionally furnished bars, well cooked food inc excellent breakfasts in cottagey dining room, and decent wines; no accommodation 25 Dec; dogs in bar only

HAROME Pheasant *Mill St, Harome, Helmsley, North Yorkshire YO62 5JG* (01439) 771241 **£92***, plus special breaks; 12 rms. Family-run hotel with a relaxed homely lounge, and traditional bar with beams, inglenook fireplace and flagstones, good very popular food, efficient service, and indoor heated swimming pool; cl Dec–Feb; children over 7; disabled access; dogs welcome in bedrooms

HAWNBY Laskill Grange *Easterside, Helmsley, York*

YO62 5NB (01439) 798268 **£59***, plus special breaks; 6 rms, some in beamy converted outside building. Attractive and welcoming creeper-covered stone house on big sheep and cattle farm nr Rievaulx Abbey; open fire, antiques and books in comfortable lounge, conservatory overlooking the garden, good food using home-grown produce, and own natural spring water; self-catering also, with a play area; cl 25 Dec; partial disabled access; dogs welcome

HELMSLEY Black Swan *Market Pl, Helmsley, North Yorkshire YO62 5BJ (01439) 770466* **£150**, plus special breaks; 45 well equipped and comfortable rms. Striking Georgian house and adjoining Tudor rectory with beamed and panelled hotel bar, attractive carved oak settles and Windsor armchairs, cosy and comfortable lounges with lots of character, and a charming sheltered garden; dogs welcome in bedrooms

KILBURN Forresters Arms *Kilburn, North Yorkshire YO61 4AH (01347) 868386* **£58***, plus special breaks; 10 clean, bright rms. Friendly old coaching inn opposite the pretty village gardens; sturdy but elegant furnishings made next door at Thompson mouse furniture workshop, big log fire in cosy lower bar, interesting Henry Dee bar in what was a stable with manger and stalls still visible, and enjoyable food in restaurant and beamed bar; disabled access; dogs welcome away from dining room

MIDDLETON Cottage Leas Country Hotel *Nova Lane, Middleton, Pickering, North Yorkshire YO18 8PN (01751) 472129* **£83**, plus special breaks; 11 comfortable newly refurbished rms. Delightful, peaceful 18th-c farmhouse with extensive gardens, comfortable informal rooms, beamed ceilings, open log fire in cosy lounge, a well stocked bar, and enjoyable creative food; partial disabled access; dogs welcome in bedrooms

THE YORKSHIRE DALES, HARROGATE & RIPON

Dog Friendly Hotels and B&Bs

BAINBRIDGE Rose & Crown *Bainbridge, Leyburn, North Yorkshire DL8 3EE (01969) 650225* **£64***, plus special breaks; 12 comfortable rms. 15th-c coaching inn overlooking lovely green, with antique settles and other old furniture in beamed and panelled front bar, open log fires, cosy residents' lounge, big wine list, and home-made traditional food in bar and restaurant; pets welcome by prior arrangement; disabled access; dogs welcome

BOLTON ABBEY Devonshire Arms *Bolton Abbey, Skipton, North Yorkshire BD23 6AJ (01756) 718111* **£195***, plus special breaks; 41 individually furnished rms with thoughtful extras. Close to the priory itself and in lovely countryside, this civilised former coaching inn owned by the Duke of Devonshire has been carefully furnished with fine antiques and paintings from Chatsworth; log fires, impeccable service, beautifully presented imaginative food in elegant restaurant, super breakfasts; health centre; children over 12 in restaurant; disabled access; dogs welcome in bedrooms

BRAFFERTON Laurel Manor Farm *Brafferton, York YO61 2NZ (01423) 360436* **£60**; 3 big beamed rms. Tall Georgian house with lovely views, surrounded by 28 acres of farmland: rare breeds, horses, fishing in the River Swale, 1,500 trees, carefully planted landscaped gardens, and croquet and tennis; open fire in comfortable sitting room, antiques and family photographs, aircraft models and pictures, good breakfasts and enjoyable candlelit family dinners using home-grown produce (by arrangement), and friendly, attentive owners; horses and other pets welcome in stable room; dogs welcome in bedrooms

BUCKDEN Buck *Buckden, Skipton, North Yorkshire BD23 5JA* (01756) 760228 **£79***, plus special breaks; 14 comfortable rms. Busy pub, popular with walkers and surrounded by moorland views; snug original area and bustling extended open-plan bar, popular food served by smartly uniformed staff in attractive no smoking dining room, decent wines, and well kept real ales; cl 2nd and 3rd wk Jan; children over 7 in restaurant; disabled access; dogs welcome in bedrooms

CRAY White Lion *Cray, Skipton, North Yorkshire BD23 5JB* (01756) 760262 **£55**, plus special breaks; 9 comfortable rms, most with showers. Welcoming little pub spectacularly isolated 335 metres (1,100 ft) up with super views, lots of walks, traditional feel with flagstones, beams and log fires, good bar food, and decent wines; dogs welcome

HARROGATE Alexa House *26 Ripon Rd, Harrogate, North Yorkshire HG1 2JJ* (01423) 501988 **£65***, plus special breaks; 13 rms, some in former stable block. Attractive Georgian house with friendly staff, comfortable lounge, good home cooking in no smoking dining room, and marvellous breakfasts; good disabled access; dogs welcome in bedrooms

KNARESBOROUGH Dower House *Bond End, Knaresborough, North Yorkshire HG5 9AL* (01423) 863302 **£89**, plus special breaks; 31 clean, comfortable rms. Creeper-clad 15th-c former dower house with attractively furnished public rooms of some character, good food in Terrace Restaurant, super breakfasts, helpful service, and leisure and health club; partial disabled access; dogs welcome in bedrooms

LONG PRESTON Maypole *Main St, Long Preston, Skipton, North Yorkshire BD23 4PH* (01729) 840219 **£49***, plus winter breaks; 6 comfortable rms. Neatly kept 17th-c pub with generous helpings of enjoyable traditional food (and nice breakfasts) in spacious beamed dining room, open fire in lounge bar, real ales, and helpful service; dogs welcome

MALHAM Miresfield Farm *Malham, Skipton, North Yorkshire BD23 4DA (01729) 830414* **£50**, plus winter breaks; 11 rms. Spacious old farmhouse with good freshly prepared food in beamed dining room, pleasant conservatory and two lounges, and lovely garden by stream and village green; cl Jan; dogs welcome in bedrooms

MARKINGTON Hob Green *Markington, Harrogate, North Yorkshire HG3 3PJ (01423) 770031* **£100***, plus special breaks; 12 well equipped pretty rms. Lovely gardens and over 800 acres of rolling countryside surround this charming 18th-c stone hotel; comfortable and pretty lounge and garden room, log fires, antique furniture, fresh flowers, relaxed atmosphere, good interesting food, decent choice of wines, and friendly service; dogs welcome in bedrooms

NEWTON-LE-WILLOWS Hall *Newton-le-Willows, Bedale, North Yorkshire DL8 1SW (01677) 450210* **£90***; 3 spacious rms. Handsome Georgian house with quiet gardens and acres of paddocks; lots of fine antiques, paintings and wall hangings, tranquil drawing room with an open fire and French windows into the garden, cosy homely snug with another fire, honesty bar, good breakfasts in light breakfast room (home-made fruitcake, tea and coffee always available), enjoyable food in elegant dining room (by prior arrangement), and a helpful and hospitable owner; children over 13 (or by arrangement); dogs welcome in the stable block by arrangement

RAMSGILL Yorke Arms *Ramsgill, Harrogate, North Yorkshire HG3 5RL (01423) 755243* **£170*** inc dinner, plus special breaks; 14 attractive rms inc a cottage on the village green. Enjoyable small former shooting lodge (now best thought of as a restaurant-with-rooms) with antique furnishings, log fires, exceptionally good imaginative cooking in comfortable dining rooms and new Beckside room, fine wines, real ales, courteous service, and lovely surrounding walks; cl last 2 wks Jan; children over 12 in dining room; dogs in cottage

RICHMOND Millgate House *Millgate, Richmond, North Yorkshire DL10 4JN (01748) 823571* **£70***; 3 rms, 2 overlooking the garden. Georgian town house with lots of interesting antiques and lovely plants, a peaceful drawing room, warm friendly owners offering meticulous attention to detail, and good breakfasts in charming dining room which also overlooks the garden; it is this award-winning small garden with views over the River Swale and the Cleveland Hills beyond, that is so special, filled with wonderful roses, ferns, clematis and hostas – they have a booklet listing the plants; children over 10; dogs welcome in bedrooms

RIPLEY Boars Head *Ripley, Harrogate, North Yorkshire HG3 3AY (01423) 771888* **£120***, plus special breaks; 25 charmingly decorated rms. In a delightful estate village, this fine old coaching inn has a relaxed, welcoming atmosphere, with comfortable sofas in attractively decorated lounges, long flagstoned bar, notable wines by the glass, fine food in bar and restful dining room, and unobtrusive service; games, videos and special menus for children; disabled access; dogs welcome in bedrooms

RIPON Ripon Spa *Park St, Ripon, North Yorkshire HG4 2BU (01765) 602172* **£95**, plus special breaks; 40 individually furnished rms, many overlooking the grounds. Neatly kept friendly and comfortable Edwardian hotel with seven acres of charming gardens, yet only a short walk from the centre; attractive public rooms, winter log fires, and good food in bar and restaurant; disabled access; dogs welcome away from eating areas

SEDBUSK Stone House *Hawes, North Yorkshire DL8 3PT (01969) 667571* **£79**, plus special breaks; 22 rms, 5 with own conservatories. Small, warmly friendly Edwardian hotel in a stunning setting with magnificent views; country-house feel and appropriate furnishings, attractive oak-panelled drawing room, billiard room, log fires, and exemplary service offering good local information; pleasant extended dining room with excellent wholesome food (special needs catered for) inc super breakfasts, and reasonable choice of wines; tennis lawn in the grounds, wonderful walks; P G Wodehouse stayed here as a guest of the original owner who employed a butler called Jeeves – it was on him that Wodehouse based his famous character; cl midweek Dec and Jan; good disabled access; dogs welcome in bedrooms

STUDLEY ROGER Lawrence House *Studley Roger, Ripon, North Yorkshire HG4 3AY (01765) 600947* **£90***; 2 spacious, lovely rms. Attractive Georgian house with two acres of lovely garden on the edge of Studley Royal and Fountains Abbey; fine antiques and pictures, log fires, good breakfasts, and delicious evening meals; cl Christmas and New Year; children by arrangement; dogs welcome in bedrooms

THORNTON WATLASS Buck *Thornton Watlass, Ripon, North Yorkshire HG4 4AH (01677) 422461* **£70***, plus fishing, racing and special breaks; 7 rms, most with own bthrm. Cheerful country pub overlooking cricket green in very

attractive village, with interesting beamed rooms, open fire, jazz Sun lunchtime twice a month, enjoyable food, and lots of nearby walks; cl pm 25 Dec; dogs welcome in bedrooms
WEST WITTON Wensleydale Heifer *West Witton, Leyburn, North Yorkshire DL8 4LS (01969) 622322* **£80***, plus special breaks; 9 rms. Friendly 17th-c coaching inn with comfortable furnishings, log fires and oak beams, and a cosy bar; good local game and fresh seafood in bistro or spacious restaurant; dogs welcome in bedrooms

WEST & SOUTH YORKSHIRE

Dog Friendly Hotels and B&Bs

BRADFORD Victoria Hotel *Bridge St, Bradford, West Yorkshire BD1 1JX (01274) 728706* **£60**w, plus special breaks; 60 well equipped rms with CD and video. Carefully renovated Victorian station hotel with many original features and lots of stylish character, bustling bar, popular and informal brasserie serving good modern food, and marvellous breakfasts, small private gym and sauna; disabled access; dogs welcome in bedrooms
HALIFAX Holdsworth House *Holmfield, Halifax, West Yorkshire HX2 9TG (01422) 240024* **£98**, plus wknd breaks; 40 traditional, individually decorated, quiet rms. Lovely, immaculately kept 17th-c house a few miles outside Halifax, with antiques, fresh flowers and fires in comfortable lounges, lots of sitting areas in the two bar rooms, friendly, particularly helpful staff, two carefully furnished dining rooms (one oak panelled) with enjoyable food and very good wine list, and garden; cl 26–30 Dec; dogs welcome in bedrooms

LEEDS 42 The Calls *Leeds, West Yorkshire LS2 7EW (0113) 244 0099* **£176.50**w, inc bottle of champagne, plus special breaks; 41 attractive rms using original features, with lots of extras, CD stereo with disc library, satellite TV and good views. Stylish modern hotel in converted riverside grain mill in peaceful spot overlooking the River Aire, with genuinely friendly staff, marvellous food in restaurant and next-door chic but informal Brasserie Forty-Four, and fine breakfasts; cl 4 days over Christmas; disabled access; dogs welcome in bedrooms

LINTON Wood Hall *Trip Lane, Linton, Wetherby, West Yorkshire LS22 4JA (01937) 587271* **£140***, plus racing breaks; 42 spacious well furnished rms. Grand Georgian mansion in over a hundred acres of parkland by the River Wharfe; comfortable reception rooms, log fire, antiques and fresh flowers, and imaginative cooking in the no smoking restaurant; indoor swimming pool and health centre; disabled access; dogs welcome in bedrooms

MONK FRYSTON Monk Fryston Hall *Main St, Monk Fryston, Leeds, West Yorkshire LS25 5DU (01977) 682369* **£109**, plus wknd and special breaks; 30 comfortable, recently refurbished rms. Benedictine manor house in 30 acres of secluded gardens with lake and woodland, an oak-panelled lounge and bar with log fires, antiques, paintings and fresh flowers, good honest food, and friendly helpful staff; disabled access; dogs welcome away from restaurant

OTLEY Chevin Lodge *Yorkgate, Otley, West Yorkshire LS21 3NU (01943) 467818* **£110**, plus special breaks; 50 rms, some in log lodges deep in the woods. Built of Finnish logs with walks through 50 acres of birchwood (lots of wildlife), this comfortable hotel has its own leisure club, good food in lakeside restaurant, and friendly service; tennis and fishing; disabled access; dogs welcome in bedrooms

York

Dog Friendly Hotels and B&Bs

YORK Dairy Guesthouse *3 Scarcroft Rd, York YO23 1ND* (01904) 639367 **£55***; 5 attractive rms, most with own bthrm. Carefully restored no smoking Victorian house with lots of original features and attention to detail, enjoyable breakfasts with vegetarian and vegan dishes, warmly hospitable atmosphere, friendly, entertaining and knowledgeable owner, and charming little flower-filled courtyard; cl mid-Dec–end Jan; disabled access; dogs welcome in bedrooms

YORK Grange Hotel *1 Clifton, York YO30 6AA* (01904) 644744 **£135**, plus special breaks; 30 individually decorated rms with antiques and chintz. Close to the Minster, this Regency town house has elegant public rooms, an open fire, newspapers, good breakfasts, excellent restaurant food (there's also a brasserie), and warmly friendly staff; car park; disabled access; dogs welcome in bedrooms

Dog Friendly Pubs

BECK HOLE
Birch Hall *Off A169 SW of Whitby, from top of Sleights Moor* Unique and charming pub-cum-village shop in great surroundings, a treasure; very simple but most unusual, with basic good value snacks, seats outside, marvellous surrounding walks – you can walk along the disused railway line from Goathland; part of the path from Beck Hole to Grosmont is surfaced with mussel shells
Free house ~ Licensee Colin Jackson ~ Real ale ~ Bar food

(available during all opening hours) ~ No credit cards ~ (01947)
896245 ~ Children in small family room ~ Dogs welcome ~
Open 11–11; 12–10.30 Sun; 11–3, 7.30–11 in winter, 12–3,
7.30–10.30 Sun in winter; closed Mon evenings

BRADFIELD

Strines Inn *From A57 heading E of junction with A6013*
(Ladybower Reservoir) take first left turn (signposted with
Bradfield) then bear left; with a map can also be reached more
circuitously from Strines signpost on A616 at head of Underbank
Reservoir, W of Stocksbridge

Isolated inn by woods and moorland, black beams liberally
decked with copper kettles and so forth, quite a menagerie
of stuffed animals, homely traditional furnishings, coal fires,
tasty bar food, good drinks; safely fenced play area with
summer bouncy castle, some rescued animals

Free house ~ Licensee Jeremy Stanish ~ Real ale ~ Bar food (all
day in summer and all day at weekends all year; no food
Mon–Thurs evenings Jan–Feb) ~ (0114) 285 1247 ~ Children in
eating area of bar until 9 ~ Dogs welcome ~ Open 10.30–11;
10.30–10.30 Sun; 10.30–3, 6–11 weekdays in winter; closed
25 Dec ~ Bedrooms: £40B/£65B

BURNSALL

Red Lion *B6160 S of Grassington, on Ilkley road; OS Sheet 98,*
map reference 033613

Fishing inn below the fells on River Wharfe, bustling
panelled main bar, log fire in front dining area, imaginative
highly enjoyable food, good wines; tables outside, good
bedrooms

Free house ~ Licensee Elizabeth Grayshon ~ Real ale ~ Bar food
(12–2.30(3 Sun), 6–9.30) ~ Restaurant ~ (01756) 720204 ~
Children welcome ~ Dogs allowed in bar and bedrooms ~ Open
11–11; 12–10.30 Sun ~ Bedrooms: £53.50B/£107B

CARLTON

Foresters Arms *Off A684 W of Leyburn, just past Wensley; or take Coverdale hill road from Kettlewell, off B6160*

Charming inn, relaxed and pubby, in a pretty village at the heart of the Yorkshire Dales, with good interesting food, a fine choice of wines and whiskies, low beams, log fires and nice bedrooms; some bench seats out among tubs of flowers with lovely views

Free house ~ Licensee Jane Martin ~ Real ale ~ Bar food (not Sun evening or Mon and Tues lunchtime) ~ Restaurant ~ (01969) 640272 ~ Children in eating area of bar ~ Dogs allowed in bar and bedrooms ~ Open 12–3, 6.30–11; 12–3, 7–10.30 Sun; closed Mon ~ Bedrooms: £40B/£75B

EAST WITTON

Blue Lion *A6108 Leyburn–Ripon*

One of Britain's very best dining pubs, with great imaginative food and good wines, but also warmly welcoming if you just pop in for a drink or a sandwich; great character, with interesting furnishings (and a friendly Labrador called Archie); picnic-sets outside look beyond the village to Witton Fell, and the bedrooms are good

Free house ~ Licensee Paul Klein ~ Real ale ~ Bar food ~ Restaurant ~ (01969) 624273 ~ Children in eating area of bar and restaurant ~ Dogs welcome ~ Open 11–11; 12–10.30 Sun ~ Bedrooms: £53.50S/£79B

HUBBERHOLME

George *Village signposted from Buckden; about 1 mile NW*

J B Priestley's favourite pub, the highest in the Dales, two neat character rooms, heavy beams, bare stone and flagstones, open stove in the big fireplace, good wholesome bar food; tables out looking over the moors and River Wharfe

Free house ~ Licensees Jenny and Terry Browne ~ Real ale ~ Bar

food (12–2, 6.30–8.45) ~ (01756) 760223 ~ Children in eating area of bar; no children under 12 to stay overnight ~ Dogs allowed in bar and bedrooms ~ Open 11–3, 6–11; 12–3, 6–10.30 Sun; closed last 3 wks Jan ~ Bedrooms: £28/£42(£56S)(£60B)

LANGTHWAITE

Charles Bathurst *Arkengarthdale, a mile N towards Tan Hill; generally known as the CB Inn*

Bleakly impressive spot, with fine views and plenty of walks; long bar with light pine furnishings and roaring fire, well kept beers, well liked food using local ingredients and cooked by the licensee; bedrooms pretty and comfortable *Free house ~ Licensees Charles and Stacy Cody ~ Real ale ~ Bar food ~ Restaurant ~ (01748) 884567 ~ Children welcome ~ Dogs welcome ~ Open 11–11; 3–11 Mon–Thurs during Dec–Feb; 12–10.30 Sun ~ Bedrooms: /£65B*

MUKER

Farmers Arms *B6270 W of Reeth*

Unpretentious friendly local, cosy and traditional, with a warm open fire and popular straightforward bar food; self-catering studio flat, rewarding walks both nearby and up over Buttertubs Pass or to the north, to Tan Hill and beyond *Free house ~ Licensees Chris and Marjorie Bellwood ~ Real ale ~ Bar food ~ No credit cards ~ (01748) 886297 ~ Children welcome ~ Dogs welcome ~ Open 11–3, 6.30–11; 12–3, 7–10.30 Sun; 11–2.30, 7–11 in winter*

WIDDOP

Pack Horse *The Ridge; from A646 on W side of Hebden Bridge, turn off at Heptonstall signpost (as it's a sharp turn, coming out of Hebden Bridge road signs direct you around a turning circle), then follow Slack and Widdop signposts; can also be reached from Nelson and Colne, on high, pretty road; OS Sheet 103, map reference 952317*

Isolated traditional pub on Heptonstall Moor, panelling, stripped stone, sturdy furnishings and warm winter fires, good beers and lots of malt whiskies, decent bar food, seats outside

Free house ~ Licensee Andrew Hollinrake ~ Real ale ~ Bar food (not Mon or wkdy winter lunchtimes) ~ Restaurant ~ (01422) 842803 ~ Children in eating area of bar ~ Dogs welcome ~ Open 12–3, 7–11; 12–11 Sun; closed wkdy winter lunchtimes and Mon ~ Bedrooms: £28S/£44B

LONDON

Dog Friendly Hotels and B&Bs

22 Jermyn Street Hotel 22 Jermyn St SW1Y 6HP (020) 7734 2353 **£272.05**; 5 rms and 13 suites – spacious with deeply comfortable seats and sofas, flowers, plants, and antiques. Stylish little hotel owned by the same family for over 80 years and much loved by customers; no public rooms but wonderful 24-hr service, helpful notes and suggestions from the friendly owners, in-room light meals, and a warm welcome for children (with their own fact sheet listing shops, restaurants, and sights geared towards them, free video library, old-fashioned and electronic games, and own bathrobes); disabled access; dogs welcome

Basil Street Hotel 8 Basil St SW3 1AH (020) 7581 3311 **£232.65**, plus special breaks; 80 pretty, decent-sized rms. Handy for Harrods and Hyde Park, this very civilised, privately owned Edwardian hotel has a relaxed atmosphere, antiques, fine carpets and paintings in the public rooms, a panelled restaurant with reliably enjoyable food, afternoon teas in lounge, and ladies' club (named after a parrot who had to go when his language became inappropriate); helpful courteous service – many of the staff have been here for years; dogs welcome in bedrooms

Capital 22–24 Basil St SW3 1AT (020) 7589 5171 **£313**; 48 luxury rms with lovely fabrics, fine paintings, marble bthrms, and tempting extras. Exclusive little hotel nr Harrods with a warm welcome and log fire in reception, intimate panelled bar with good nibbles, a small lounge, exemplary service, and exceptional French-inspired food in chandelier-lit restaurant; disabled access; dogs welcome in bedrooms

Chesterfield 35 Charles St W1X 8LX (020) 7491 2622 **£264.37**, plus special breaks; 110 well equipped and newly refurbished pretty rms. Charming hotel just off Berkeley Sq, with particularly courteous helpful staff, afternoon tea in panelled library, a relaxed club-style bar with resident pianist, and fine food in attractive restaurant or light and airy conservatory; dogs welcome in bedrooms

Conrad London Chelsea Harbour SW10 0XG (020) 7823 3000 **£180**; 160 luxury suites with a light and spacious living room area (many have sofa-beds so two small children could stay with parents at no extra cost). London's first 'suite hotel', tucked away in the quiet modern enclave of the Chelsea Harbour development and overlooking its small marina; enjoyable Mediterranean and Asian-influenced dishes in Aquasia restaurant and bar, friendly service, and health club; disabled access; dogs welcome (if small)

Halkin 5 Halkin St SW1X 7DJ (020) 7333 1000 **£270**w, plus special breaks; 41 stylish well equipped rms, with wonderful marble bthrms. Despite its Georgian exterior, the décor and furnishings here are ultra-modern but enjoyable, and there's a particularly good Thai restaurant overlooking the garden; fine breakfasts, and really charming staff; much liked by businessmen, too; disabled access; dogs if very well trained and by prior arrangement

Hazlitts *6 Frith St W1V 5TZ (020) 7434 1771* **£229.13**, plus special breaks; 23 rms with 18th- or 19th-c beds and free-standing Victorian baths with early brass shower mixer units. Behind a typically Soho façade of listed early Georgian houses, this well kept and comfortably laid-out little hotel has been completely restored this year; very handy for the West End; good continental breakfasts served in your bedroom, snacks in the sitting room, lots of restaurants all around; kind, helpful service; dogs by prior arrangement

L'Hotel *28 Basil St SW3 1AS (020) 7589 6286* **£164.50**; 12 well equipped rms. Small family-owned French-style city hotel, nr Harrods, and set above the neatly kept well run Metro wine bar where continental breakfasts are served – as well as good modern French café food; friendly staff; disabled access; dogs by prior arrangement

Swiss House *171 Old Brompton Rd SW5 0AN (020) 7373 2769* **£93**; 15 rms. Festooned with ivy and flower boxes, this is a warmly friendly and good value family-run hotel, relaxed and tidy inside, with very good buffet continental breakfasts – English available, too; dogs welcome in bedrooms

SCOTLAND
EAST SCOTLAND

Dog Friendly Hotels and B&Bs

ARDEONAIG **Ardeonaig Hotel** *Ardeonaig, Killin, Perthshire FK21 8SY* (01567) 820400 **£100**; 12 rms. Extended 17th-c farmhouse on S shore of Loch Tay with log fire in snug and lounge, library with fine views, and tasty, honest food using fresh local produce; salmon fishing rights on the loch – as well as fishing for trout and char – a drying and rod room, and boats and outboards; shooting, stalking and pony trekking can be arranged, lots of surrounding walks; cl 2 wks at Christmas and 2 wks early Jan; dogs welcome in bedrooms

AUCHTERARDER **Gleneagles Hotel** *Auchterarder, Perthshire PH3 1NF* (01764) 662231 **£320***, plus special breaks; 275 individually decorated rms. Grand hotel in lovely surroundings with attractive gardens and outstanding leisure facilities: three championship golf courses (one designed by Jack Nicklaus), shooting, riding, fishing, health spa, tennis, squash, croquet and even falconry, lots of children's activities inc playroom with arts and crafts; comfortable, elegant high-ceilinged day rooms, a fine bar, exceptional service, pianists, enjoyable food using local produce (much is home-grown) in four restaurants, famous afternoon teas; disabled access; dogs welcome in bedrooms

AVIEMORE **Lynwilg House** *Aviemore, Inverness-shire PH22 1PZ* (01479) 811685 **£60**; 4 rms, 3 with shower. Attractive, quietly set 1930s-style house in four acres of landscaped gardens with open fire in spacious lounge, lovely breakfasts with their own free-range eggs and home-baked bread, super dinners using home-grown produce, and charming owners; plenty to do nearby; cl Nov–Dec; dogs welcome

BALLATER Auld Kirk *31 Braemar Rd, Ballater, Aberdeenshire AB35 5RQ (01339) 755762* **£60**, plus winter breaks; 7 attractive rms, inc 2 family rms. 19th-c church converted to a hotel in 1990, still with bell tower, stained glass and exposed rafters; original pillared pine ceiling in newly refurbished restaurant, other public rooms with homely décor; cl 25–27 Dec, 1–4 Jan; dogs welcome in bedrooms

BALLATER Balgonie Country House *Braemar Pl, Ballater, Aberdeenshire AB35 5NQ (01339) 755482* **£125***, plus special breaks; 9 pretty rms. Quietly set and spotless Edwardian house with fine views from four acres of mature gardens, particularly helpful friendly owners, fresh flowers, games and books in lounges, and most enjoyable food using the best local produce in charming dining room; cl 6 Jan–10 Feb; dogs by arrangement

BLAIRGOWRIE Kinloch House *Blairgowrie, Perthshire PH10 6SG (01250) 884237* **£175***, plus special breaks; 20 individually decorated rms. Creeper-covered 19th-c country house in 25 acres of parkland with Highland cattle and fine views; relaxed lounges, comfortable bar, pretty conservatory with lots of plants, and fine choice of carefully prepared food in an elegant dining room; popular sportsmen's room with own entrance, drying facilities, gun cupboard, freezer, game larder and so forth, and new fitness suite; cl 16–30 Dec; children over 7 in dining room; disabled access; dogs welcome in bedrooms

BRIDGE OF CALLY Bridge of Cally Hotel *Bridge of Cally, Blairgowrie, Perthshire PH10 7JJ (01250) 886231* **£50**, plus winter breaks; 18 rms. In an acre of grounds along the

River Ardle, this former drovers' inn is a friendly family-run place with good value home-made food using seasonal game in restaurant and comfortable bar; dogs welcome

CALLANDER Poppies *Leny Rd, Callander, Perthshire FK17 8AL (01877) 330329* **£60***; 9 rms. Small private hotel with excellent food in popular and attractive candlelit dining room, comfortable lounge, helpful friendly owners, and seats in the garden; cl Jan; dogs welcome

DALCROSS Easter Dalziel Farm *Dalcross, Inverness-shire IV2 7JL (01667) 462213* **£44***; 3 rms with shared bthrm. Early Victorian farmhouse on 210 acres of family-run mixed farm (beef cattle and grain) with friendly helpful owners, log fire in lounge, good Scottish breakfasts in big dining room and – when farm commitments allow – evening meal using own beef, lamb and veg; self-catering cottages, too; cl Christmas and New Year; dogs welcome

DUNBLANE Cromlix House *Cromlix, Dunblane, Perthshire FK15 9JT (01786) 822125* **£215***, plus special breaks; 14 rms inc 8 spacious suites. Walking, loch and river fishing or shooting on 2,000 acres around this rather gracious country house; relaxing day rooms with fine antiques and family portraits, an informal atmosphere, very good food using local produce in two dining rooms, and courteous service; cl Jan; dogs welcome in bedrooms

EAST HAUGH East Haugh House *East Haugh, Pitlochry, Tayside PH16 5TE (01796) 473121* **£100*** inc dinner, plus special breaks; 12 rms, 5 in converted bothy, some with four-posters and one with open fire. Turreted stone house with lots of character, delightful conservatory bar, house-party atmosphere and very good food inc local seafood and game in season cooked by chef/proprietor; excellent shooting, stalking and salmon and trout fishing on surrounding local estates; cl 20–27 Dec; disabled access to one room; dogs welcome in bedrooms

FINTRY Culcreuch Castle *Fintry, Glasgow G63 0LW* *(01360) 860228* **£124***, plus special breaks; 13 individually decorated rms with lovely views. Central Scotland's oldest inhabited castle, nearly 700 years old, in beautiful 1,600-acre parkland and surrounding hills and moors, with log fires and antiques in the public rooms, good freshly prepared food in candlelit panelled dining room, and a friendly relaxed atmosphere, play area; 8 modern Scandinavian holiday lodges, too; disabled access; dogs by arrangement

GLENDEVON Tormaukin *Glendevon, Dollar, Clackman-nanshire FK14 7JY (01259) 781252* **£90**, plus special breaks; 12 comfortable rms, some in converted stable block. Neatly kept 18th-c inn in good walking country, with loch and river fishing, lots of golf courses in reach, beamed dining room and softly lit bar, very good food using fresh local produce (soup and coffee all day), and fine breakfasts, also a self-catering chalet; cl 4 days beginning of Jan; disabled access; dogs welcome in bedrooms

GLENROTHES Balbirnie House *Markinch, Glenrothes, Fife KY7 6NE (01592) 610066* **£190***, plus special breaks; 30 rms. Fine Georgian country house in 400-acre park landscaped in Capability Brown style, with fresh flowers, open fires and antiques in gracious public rooms, extremely good inventive food, and a big wine list; disabled access; dogs welcome in bedrooms

INVERNESS Bunchrew House *Bunchrew, Inverness IV3 8TA (01463) 234917* **£155**, plus special breaks; 14 individually decorated rms. Friendly 17th-c mansion W of town by Beauly Firth with fine views and landscaped gardens, log fire in the elegant panelled drawing room, and traditional cooking using local produce and local game and venison; cl 22–26 Dec; dogs welcome in bedrooms

INVERNESS Dunain Park *Inverness IV3 8JN (01463) 230512* **£158**; 13 rms inc 6 suites with own lounge. 19th-c Italianate mansion in six acres of well tended gardens and woodland, overlooking the River Ness and Caledonian Canal; charming owners, traditional homely décor with family photographs and china ornaments, log fires and fresh flowers, wonderful food using home-grown produce and local game, fish and Aberdeen Angus meat, generous breakfasts, and 200 whiskies; small warm swimming pool, sauna, lots of walks and golf courses nearby; disabled access; dogs welcome in bedrooms

KINCLAVEN BY STANLEY Ballathie House *Stanley, Perth PH1 4QN (01250) 883268* **£160**, plus special breaks; 42 pretty rms, some luxurious and some in new building with river views from balconies. On a vast estate with fine salmon fishing on the River Tay (lodges and facilities for fishermen) and plenty of sporting opportunities, this turreted mansion has a comfortable and relaxed drawing room, separate lounge and bar, good enjoyable modern Scottish cooking, croquet and putting; disabled access; dogs welcome in bedrooms

KINNESSWOOD Lomond Country Inn *Main St, Kinnesswood, Kinross KY13 9HN (01592) 840253* **£70***; 10 comfortable rms, 8 in an extension. Attractive little inn in village centre with views across Loch Leven (nice sunsets), open fires, informal bustling bar, well kept real ales, and good reasonably priced bar and restaurant food using local produce; disabled access; dogs welcome in bedrooms

KIRKTON OF GLENISLA Glenisla Hotel *Glenisla, Blairgowrie, Perthshire PH11 8PH (01575) 582223* **£50**; 6 rms.

Attractively placed peaceful 17th-c coaching inn, prettily restored with natural unpainted wood throughout, happily unmatched furniture, bar with open fire and two real ales, good food, cheerful warm atmosphere; nice garden; cl 25–26 Dec; dogs welcome in bedrooms

NAIRN Clifton House *Viewfield St, Nairn, Nairnshire IV12 4HW* (01667) 453119 **£100***; 12 individually decorated comfortable rms. Lovely, civilised, flower-filled old family hotel (the present owner has lived in this elegant Victorian house all his life and has been running it as a hotel since 1952), individually furnished with exquisite antiques, paintings and sculptures; extremely good food using local eggs, fish, meat and game, fine breakfasts with home-made jams, bread and oatcakes, and an exceptional wine list; during the winter they stage some 20 concerts, plays and recitals; cl mid-Dec–mid-Jan; dogs welcome in bedrooms

PEAT INN Peat Inn *Peat Inn, Cupar, Fife KY15 5LH* (01334) 840206 **£150***, plus special breaks; 8 luxurious suites. Famous restaurant with rooms: beams and white plaster walls, log fires and comfortable sofas, friendly service, fine interesting food using the best local produce inc plenty of game and seafood, and an excellent wine list; cl Sun and Mon, 25 Dec, 1 Jan; disabled access; dogs welcome in bedrooms

PITLOCHRY Killiecrankie Hotel *Killiecrankie, Pitlochry, Perthshire PH16 5LG* (01796) 473220 **£190*** inc dinner, plus special breaks; 10 spotless rms. Comfortable country hotel in spacious grounds with splendid mountain views, mahogany-panelled bar with stuffed animals and fine wildlife paintings, cosy sitting room with books and games, a relaxed atmosphere, friendly newish owners, and excellent well presented, locally sourced food in elegant restaurant; cl 3

Jan–13 Feb; disabled access; dogs welcome in bedrooms

SCONE Murrayshall House *Perth PH2 7PH (01738) 551171* **£130***, plus special breaks; 41 rms inc 14 suites, plus lodge which sleeps 6. Handsome mansion in 300-acre park, very popular with golfers (it has two of its own courses); comfortable elegant public rooms, warm friendly staff, relaxed atmosphere, imaginative food, and good wines; disabled access; dogs welcome

SPEAN BRIDGE Letterfinlay Lodge *Letterfinlay, Spean Bridge, Inverness-shire PH34 4DZ (01397) 712622* **£80***, plus special breaks; 13 rms, most with own bthrm. Secluded and genteel family-run country house right on the edge of our East Scotland area and well placed for the West too, with picture window in extensive modern bar overlooking loch; elegantly panelled small cocktail bar, good popular food, friendly attentive service; grounds run down through rhododendrons to the jetty and Loch Lochy; fishing can be arranged; cl Nov–Mar; dogs welcome in bedrooms

SPITTAL OF GLENSHEE Dalmunzie House *Glenshee, Blairgowrie, Perthshire PH10 7QG (01250) 885224* **£100**, plus special breaks; 16 rms with own bthrm. Old-fashioned former Victorian shooting lodge, off A93, peacefully set in huge estate among spectacular mountains, plenty of walks within it, and own golf course; family-run atmosphere, enjoyable food using local produce, and tasty breakfasts; cl Dec; dogs welcome in bedrooms

TOMINTOUL Argyle House *7 Main St, Tomintoul, Ballindalloch, Banffshire AB37 9EX (01807) 580766* **£32***; 5 rms, most with own bthrm. Small family run guesthouse, originally a Temperance Hotel, and recently carefully renovated; library with books for guests to borrow, good breakfasts in dining room, and a genuine welcome from the friendly owners; lots to do nearby; dogs welcome in bedrooms

NORTH SCOTLAND

Dog Friendly Hotels and B&Bs

ACHILTIBUIE Summer Isles Hotel *Achiltibuie, Ullapool, Ross-shire IV26 2YQ* (01854) 622282 **£110***; 13 comfortable rms. Beautifully placed above the sea towards the end of a very long and lonely road; warm, friendly, well furnished hotel with delicious set menus using fresh ingredients (in which it's largely self-sufficient), a choice of superb puddings and excellent array of uncommon cheeses; pretty watercolours and flowers; cl mid-Oct–Easter; children over 6; dogs welcome in bedrooms

APPLECROSS Applecross Inn *Shore St, Applecross, Strathcarron, Ross-shire IV54 8LR* (01520) 744262 **£64***; 7 rms, all with breathtaking sea views over Sound of Raasay, some with shared bthrms. Gloriously placed informal inn with tables out by shore, simple comfortable and friendly bar, log or peat fire in lounge, small restaurant with excellent fresh fish and seafood; cl 25 Dec and 1 Jan; dogs welcome

CROMARTY Royal *Marine Terrace, Cromarty, Ross-shire IV11 8YN* (01381) 600217 **£59.90***; 10 rms. Traditional waterfront hotel with friendly owners and staff, attractive lounges, bars and sun lounge, and Scottish dishes in dining room; gets very busy in summer; dogs welcome in bedrooms

DRUMNADROCHIT Polmaily House *Drumnadrochit, Inverness IV63 6XT* (01456) 450343 **£115***, plus special breaks; 11 light, pretty rms. Very relaxing and homely hotel in 18 acres, with comfortable drawing room and library, open fires, and excellent food in the no smoking restaurant (wonderful packed lunches too); a happy place for families with well equipped indoor play area with lots of supervised activities, baby-sitting and -listening, hundreds of children's videos, plenty of ponies and pets, swimming pool, tennis, croquet, fishing and boating; cl 4 days at Christmas; disabled access; dogs welcome in bedrooms

GARVE Inchbae Lodge *Garve, Ross-shire IV23 2PH (01997) 455269* **£70***, plus special breaks; 15 rms, some in chalet. Former hunting lodge in lovely Highland setting with comfortable homely lounges, winter log fires, small bar (liked by locals), and good fixed-price evening meals using fresh local produce; lots of wildlife, marvellous walks; cl Christmas; disabled access; dogs welcome

GLENELG Glenelg Inn *Kirkton, Glenelg, Kyle, Ross-shire IV40 8JR (01599) 522273* **£120*** inc dinner, plus special breaks; 6 individually decorated and comfortable rms, all with fine views. Overlooking Skye across its own beach, this carefully refurbished homely hotel has a relaxed bar, comfortable sofas and blazing fires, friendly staff and locals, good food using local venison, local hill-bred lamb and lots of wonderfully fresh fish and seafood, and quite a few whiskies; the drive to the inn involves spectacular views from the steep road (and the pretty drive to Glen Beag broch is nice); open in winter if pre-booked; disabled access; dogs welcome away from dining room

ISLE ORNSAY Eilean Iarmain *Isle Ornsay, Isle of Skye IV43 8QR (01471) 833332* **£120***, plus winter breaks; 17 individual rms (those in main hotel best), all with fine views. Sparkling white hotel with Gaelic-speaking staff and locals, big cheerfully busy bar, pretty dining room with lovely sea views, and very good food; disabled access; dogs welcome in bedrooms

ISLE ORNSAY Kinloch Lodge *Isle Ornsay, Isle of Skye IV43 8QY (01471) 833214* **£150**, plus winter breaks; 14 rms. Surrounded by rugged mountain scenery at the head of Loch Na Dal, this charming white stone hotel has a relaxed atmosphere in its comfortable and attractive drawing rooms, antiques, portraits, flowers, log fires, and good imaginative food; cookery demonstrations; children by arrangement; cl 22–27 Dec; dogs welcome in bedrooms

LAIDE Old Smiddy *Laide, Achnasheen, Ross-shire IV22 2NB (01445) 731425* **£70***; 3 pretty rms with thoughtful extras. Really welcoming charming no smoking cottage in lovely spot by sea and mountains, with blazing fire in comfortable homely lounge, and dining room with super breakfasts and delicious evening meals (using local and home-grown produce; bring your own wine); lots of outside pursuits; cl Nov–Easter; children over 12; dogs welcome

PORTREE Rosedale *Quay Brae, Portree, Isle of Skye IV51 9DB (01478) 613131* **£90***, plus special breaks; 23 rms, many with harbour views. Built from three fishermen's cottages with lots of passages and stairs, this waterfront hotel has two traditional lounges, small first-floor restaurant with freshly cooked popular food, lots of whiskies in the cocktail bar, helpful staff, marvellous views; cl Nov–Easter; dogs welcome in bedrooms

RAASAY Isle of Raasay Hotel *Isle of Raasay, Kyle, Ross-shire IV40 8PB (01478) 660222* **£58***; 12 rms, the new owners plan to redecorate in 2003. Victorian hotel with marvellous views over the Sound of Raasay to Skye, popular with walkers and bird-watchers, home-made food with an emphasis on fresh fish; no petrol on the island; disabled access; dogs welcome in bedrooms

SCARISTA Scarista House *Scarista, Harris, Isle of Harris HS3 3HX (01859) 550238* **£135***, plus special breaks; 5 rms, some in annexe. Marvellously wild countryside and empty beaches surround this isolated small hotel with its antiques-furnished rooms, open fires, warm friendly atmosphere, plenty of books and records (no radio or TV), an impressive wine list, and good food in candlelit dining room using organic home-grown vegetables and herbs, hand-made cheeses, their own eggs, home-made bread, cakes, biscuits, yoghurt and marmalade, and lots of fish and shellfish; excellent for wildlife, walks and fishing; cl Christmas and occasionally in winter; dogs welcome

SCOURIE Scourie Hotel *Scourie, Lairg, Sutherland IV27 4SX (01971) 502396* **£80**, plus special breaks; 20 rms with views to Scourie Bay. A haven for anglers, with 36 exclusive beats on 25,000-acre estate; snug bar, two comfortable lounges and good food using plenty of local game and fish in smart no smoking dining room; cl mid-Oct–Mar; dogs welcome

SHIEL BRIDGE Kintail Lodge *Glenshiel, Kyle, Ross-shire IV40 8HL (01599) 511275* **£80**; 12 good value big rms. Pleasantly informal and fairly simple former shooting lodge on Loch Duich, with magnificent views, four acres of walled gardens, residents' lounge bar and comfortable sitting room, good well prepared food inc wild salmon, and fine collection of malt whiskies; dogs welcome in bedrooms

SHIELDAIG Tigh an Eilean *Shieldaig, Strathcarron, Ross-shire IV54 8XN (01520) 755251* **£110**, plus special breaks; 11 rms. Attractive hotel in outstanding position with lovely view of pine-covered island and sea, kayaks, private fishing and sea fishing arranged, within easy reach of NTS Torridon Estate, Beinn Eighe nature reserve and Applecross peninsula; pretty woodburner in one of two comfortable residents' lounges with well stocked honesty bar, modern dining room with delicious food inc home-baked bread, warmly friendly owners; cl end Oct–Mar; dogs welcome in bedrooms

SKEABOST Skeabost Country House *Skeabost Bridge, Portree, Isle of Skye IV51 9NR (01470) 532202* **£105***, plus special breaks; 19 rms, 4 in annexe in Garden House. Smart and friendly little hotel in 29 acres of landscaped grounds on the shores of Loch Snizort; 9-hole 18-tee golf course and 8 miles of salmon and trout fishing; log fires, comfortable day rooms, friendly, helpful staff, and good, enjoyable food; disabled access; dogs by arrangement

STRONTIAN Kilcamb Lodge Hotel *Strontian, Acharacle, Argyll PH36 4HY (01967) 402257* **£115***, plus winter breaks; 11 rms. Warm friendly little hotel in 28 acres by Loch Sunart, with log fires in two lounges, carefully cooked food using fresh ingredients from organic kitchen garden, fine choice of malt whiskies in small bar, and a relaxed atmosphere; beach, fishing boat, four moorings and jetty; no children; disabled access in cottage; dogs welcome in bedrooms

TORRIDON Loch Torridon Hotel *Torridon, Achnasheen, Ross-shire IV22 2EY (01445) 791242* **£132***, plus special breaks; 20 comfortable rms. Built in 1887 as a shooting lodge in 58 acres at the foot of Ben Damph by Upper Loch Torridon, this turreted stone house has unusual ornate ceilings and panelling, log fires and innovative cooking; they also run the Ben Damph Lodge nearby; cl Jan; children over 10 in dining room; disabled access; dogs welcome in bedrooms

SOUTH SCOTLAND

Dog Friendly Hotels and B&Bs

AUCHENCAIRN Balcary Bay *Auchencairn, Castle Douglas, Kirkcudbrightshire DG7 1QZ (01556) 640217* **£112***, plus special breaks; 20 rms with fine views. Once a smugglers' haunt, this charming and much liked hotel has wonderful views over the bay, neat grounds running down to the water, comfortable public rooms (one with log fire), a relaxed friendly atmosphere, good enjoyable food inc super breakfasts, and lots of walks; cl 1 Dec–1 Mar; disabled access; dogs welcome in bedrooms

BEATTOCK Auchen Castle *Beattock, Moffat, Dumfriesshire DG10 9SH (01683) 300407* **£95**; 25 pleasantly decorated rms, most with own bthrms, some in Lodge. Smart but friendly country-house hotel in lovely quiet spot with a trout loch and spectacular hill views, good food, and peaceful comfortable bar; dogs welcome in bedrooms

CANONBIE Riverside *Canonbie, Dumfriesshire DG14 0UX (013873) 71512* **£70**, plus special breaks; 7 chintzy rms, 2 in cottage. Civilised little inn with friendly owners, comfortable communicating bar rooms, open fire, attractive furnishings, good imaginative food using top-quality produce, a fine wine list, and marvellous breakfasts; cl first 2 wks Feb; partal disabled access; dogs welcome in bedrooms

EDINBURGH Balmoral Hotel *1 Princes St, Edinburgh EH2 2EQ (0131) 556 2414* **£230***, plus special breaks; 188 luxurious rms. In city centre and handy for visitor attractions. Splendid Victorian hotel with wonderfully opulent entrance hall, elegant day rooms, lovely flowers, particularly friendly helpful staff, and very good food in several restaurants; excellent leisure facilities; good disabled access; dogs welcome in bedrooms

EDINBURGH Malmaison *1 Tower Pl, Leith, Edinburgh EH6 7DB (0131) 555 6868* **£141.50***, plus special breaks; 101 stylish rms with CD players and satellite TV. Converted baronial-style seamen's mission in the fashionable docks area of Leith with very good food in the downstairs French brasserie, cheerful café bar, gym, and friendly service; free parking; disabled access; dogs welcome in bedrooms

EDINBURGH Seven Danube Street *7 Danube Street, Edinburgh EH4 1NN (0131) 332 2755* **£90**, 3 fine rms with plenty of extras. Quietly placed Georgian house with charming helpful owners, comfortable lounge, a relaxed homely atmosphere, marvellous breakfasts served at one big table, and small garden; no smoking; cl Christmas; dogs by arrangement

ESKDALEMUIR Hart Manor *Eskdalemuir, Langholm, Dumfriesshire DG13 0QQ (01387) 373217* **£83***, plus special breaks; 4 recently refurbished rms. 19th-c shooting lodge with lovely views and fine hill-walking country all around; a warm, relaxed atmosphere in lounge and library, particularly good individual and totally home-made country cooking, a thoughtful wine list and choice of malt whiskies, and superb breakfasts; no smoking; cl Christmas; children over 12; dogs welcome in bedrooms

GATEHOUSE OF FLEET Cally Palace *Gatehouse of Fleet, Castle Douglas, Kirkcudbrightshire DG7 2DL (01557) 814341* **£136** inc dinner; plus special breaks; 56 rms. 18th-c country mansion, a hotel since 1934, with marble fireplaces and ornate ceilings in the public rooms, relaxed cocktail bar, enjoyable food in elegant dining room (smart dress required), evening pianist and Sat evening dinner dance, helpful friendly staff, 18-hole golf course, croquet and tennis, indoor leisure complex with heated swimming pool, private fishing/boating loch; cl Jan, cl wkdys in Feb; disabled access; dogs welcome in bedrooms

GIFFORD Tweeddale Arms *Gifford, Haddington, East Lothian EH41 4QU (01620) 810240* **£65**, plus special breaks; 16 rms. Civilised late 17th-c inn in quiet village, with comfortable sofas and chairs in tranquil lounge, gracious dining room, wide choice of good daily-changing food, and charming service; cl 1 Jan; disabled access; dogs welcome in bedrooms

GLASGOW One Devonshire Gardens *Glasgow G12 0UX (0141) 339 2001* **£244**; 29 opulent rms. Elegant cosseting hotel a little way out from the centre, with luxurious Victorian furnishings, fresh flowers, exemplary staff, and fine modern cooking in the stylish restaurant; dogs welcome in bedrooms

GULLANE Greywalls *Duncar Rd, Gullane, East Lothian EH31 2EG (01620) 842144* **£240***, plus special breaks; 23 individually decorated rms. Overlooking Muirfield golf course, this beautiful family-run Lutyens house has antiques, open fires and flowers in its comfortable lounges and panelled library, very good food and fine wines in the restaurant, impeccable service, and lovely Gertrude Jekyll garden, all of a piece with the perfect design of the house; cl Nov–Mar; disabled access; dogs welcome in bedrooms

INNERLEITHEN Traquair Arms *Innerleithen, Peeblesshire EH44 6PD (01896) 830229* **£70**, plus special breaks; 15 comfortable rms. Very friendly hotel with interesting choice of good food in attractive dining room, cosy lounge bar, friendly service, superb local Traquair ale, and nice breakfasts; disabled access; dogs welcome away from restaurant

LOCKERBIE Dryfesdale Hotel *Dryfebridge, Lockerbie, Dumfriesshire DG11 2SF (01576) 202427* **£85**, plus wknd breaks; 16 rms, 6 on ground floor. Relaxed and comfortable former manse in five acres, open fire in homely lounge, good food in pleasant restaurant, garden and lovely surrounding countryside, putting and croquet; cl 26 Dec; good disabled access; dogs welcome in bedrooms

MELROSE Burts *Market Sq, Melrose, Roxburghshire TD6 9PN (01896) 822285* **£94***, plus special breaks; 20 rms. Welcoming 18th-c family-run hotel close to abbey ruins in delightfully quiet village; coal fire in bustling bar, residents' lounge, consistently popular imaginative food, exceptional breakfasts; cl 26 Dec; dogs welcome

MINNIGAFF Creebridge House *Creebridge, Newton Stewart, Wigtownshire DG8 6NP (01671) 402121* **£108***, plus special breaks; 19 rms inc 2 with four-posters. Attractive country-house hotel in three acres of gardens with relaxed friendly atmosphere, open fire in comfortable newly decorated drawing room, cheerful bar, and big choice of delicious food inc fine local fish and seafood in newly refurbished garden restaurant; cl 25 and 26 Dec; dogs welcome in bedrooms

NENTHORN Whitehill Farm *Nenthorn, Kelso, Roxburghshire TD5 7RZ (01573) 470203* **£48***; 4 rms, 3 with shared bthrm. Comfortable farmhouse on mixed farm with fine views, big garden, log fire in sitting room, and good home cooking; no babies; cl Christmas and New Year; dogs welcome

PEEBLES Cringletie House *Cringletie, Peebles EH45 8PL (01721) 730233* **£140**, plus special breaks; 14 pretty rms. Surrounded by 28 acres of garden and woodland and with fine views, very welcoming quiet turreted baronial mansion, delicious food using home-grown vegetables, extensive Scottish breakfasts, and excellent service; dogs welcome in bedrooms

PORTPATRICK Knockinaam Lodge *Portpatrick, Stranraer, Wigtownshire DG9 9AD (01776) 810471* **£250** inc dinner, plus special breaks; 10 individual rms. Lovely very neatly kept little hotel with comfortable pretty rooms, open fires, wonderful food, and friendly caring service; dramatic surroundings, with lots of fine cliff walks; children over 12 in evening restaurant (high tea at 6pm); dogs welcome in bedrooms

SWINTON Wheatsheaf *Main St, Swinton, Duns, Berwickshire TD11 3JJ (01890) 860257* **£85***, plus special breaks; 8 rms with baths or showers. Warmly friendly inn with exceptionally good food, a pleasantly decorated and relaxed main lounge plus small pubby area, new reception lounge, and no smoking front conservatory; garden play area for children; cl 25 Dec, 1 Jan, 2 wks Jan and 1 wk July; dogs welcome in bedrooms

WEST SCOTLAND

Dog Friendly Hotels and B&Bs

ARDUAINE Loch Melfort Hotel *Arduaine, Oban, Argyll PA34 4XG (01852) 200233* **£118**, plus special breaks; 27 rms, gorgeous sea views. Comfortable hotel popular in summer with passing yachtsmen (hotel's own moorings), nautical charts and marine glasses in airy modern bar, own lobster pots and nets so emphasis on seafood, pleasant foreshore walks, outstanding springtime woodland gardens; disabled access; dogs welcome in bedrooms

CRINAN Crinan Hotel *Crinan, Lochgilphead, Argyll PA31*

8SR (01546) 830261 **£210*** inc dinner, plus special breaks; 20 rms. Rather smart hotel by start of canal to Lochgilphead, marvellous views from stylish formal top-floor restaurant and bedrooms, nautical decorations in lounge bar, lots of local fish and large wine list; cl Christmas and New Year; disabled access; dogs welcome in bedrooms

DERVAIG Druimard Country House *Dervaig, Tobermory, Isle of Mull PA75 6QW (01688) 400345* **£125** inc dinner, plus special breaks; 7 rms. Peaceful Victorian country house with wonderful views across the glen and River Bellart, friendly helpful owners, comfortable lounge and conservatory, lots of pictures, books and magazines, good breakfasts, excellent food using the best local produce; the Mull Little Theatre is in the grounds; cl Nov–Mar; disabled access; dogs welcome in bedrooms

ELLANBEICH Inshaig Park *Easdale, Oban, Argyll PA34 4RF (01852) 300256* **£70***, plus special breaks; 6 rms. Solid family-run stone building on Seil island (bridge to mainland), a hotel since Victorian times, with stunning sea views, good food inc fresh local seafood, friendly bar and warm welcome; dogs welcome in bedrooms

ERISKA Isle of Eriska Hotel *Ledaig, Oban, Argyll PA37 1SD (01631) 720371* **£225**, plus winter breaks; 17 rms. In a wonderful position on small island linked by bridge to mainland, impressive baronial hotel with very relaxed country-house atmosphere, log fires and pretty drawing room, excellent food, exemplary service, and comprehensive wine list; leisure complex with indoor swimming pool, sauna, gym and so forth, lovely surrounding walks, 9-hole golf course, clay pigeon shooting – and plenty of wildlife inc tame badgers who come nightly to the library door for their bread and milk; cl Jan; children over 5 in pool and evening restaurant (high tea provided); disabled access; dogs welcome in bedrooms

GIGHA Gigha Hotel *Isle of Gigha PA41 7AA (01583) 505254* **£90**, plus special breaks; 13 rms, most with own bthrm. Traditional family-run hotel, small and attractive with lots of charm, bustling bar (popular with yachtsmen and locals), neatly kept comfortable residents' lounge, and local seafood in restaurant; self-contained cottages too; dogs welcome in bedrooms

KILCHRENAN Taychreggan Hotel *Kilchrenan, Taynuilt, Argyll PA35 1HQ (01866) 833211* **£127***, plus special breaks; 19 rms. Civilised and extensively refurbished hotel with fine garden running down to Loch Awe, comfortable airy bar, attractively served lunchtime bar food, polite efficient staff, good freshly prepared food in no smoking dining room, careful wine list, dozens of malt whiskies, and pretty inner courtyard; no children; dogs welcome in bedrooms

KILNINVER Knipoch *Knipoch, Oban, Argyll PA34 4QT (01852) 316251* **£144**, plus winter breaks; 20 rms. Elegant very well kept Georgian hotel in lovely countryside overlooking Loch Feochan; fine family portraits, log fires, fresh flowers and polished furniture in comfortable lounges and bars, carefully chosen wines and malt whiskies, and marvellous food inc their own smoked salmon; dogs welcome in bedrooms

ONICH Allt-Nan-Ros *Onich, Fort William, Inverness-shire PH33 6RY (01855) 821210* **£105***, plus special breaks; 20 rms, many with views over the gardens to the water. Victorian shooting lodge with fine Scottish food, friendly atmosphere, bright airy rooms, and magnificent views across Loch Linnhe and the gardens; cl 5 Jan–10 Feb; disabled access; dogs away from eating areas

PORT APPIN Airds Hotel *Port Appin, Appin, Argyll PA38*

4DF (01631) 730236 **£300*** inc dinner, plus winter breaks; 12 lovely rms – also, 4 cheaper rooms in Linnhe House 60 yds away. Instantly relaxing 18th-c inn with lovely views of Loch Linnhe and the islands of Lismore, blissfully comfortable day rooms, professional courteous staff, and charming owners; the food is exceptional (as is the wine list) and there are lots of surrounding walks, with more on Lismore (small boat every hour); cl 17–27 Dec, 6–31 Jan; dogs welcome in bedrooms

TARBERT Columba Hotel *East Pier Rd, Tarbert, Argyll PA29 6UF* (01880) 820808 **£73.90**, plus special winter breaks; 10 rms. In a peaceful position on Loch Fyne with views of the surrounding hills, this family-run hotel has log fires in the friendly bar and lounge, an informal and relaxed atmosphere, very enjoyable food using fresh local produce, and quite a few malt whiskies; cl 24–26 Dec; dogs welcome in bedrooms

TARBERT Stonefield Castle *Stonefield, Tarbert, Argyll PA29 6YJ* (01880) 820836 **£170** inc dinner, plus special breaks; 33 rms. With wonderful views and surrounding wooded grounds, this Scottish baronial mansion has comfortable public rooms and decent restaurant food; snooker room; dogs welcome in bedrooms

Dog Friendly Pubs

ABOYNE
Boat *Charlestown Road (B968, just off A93)*
Convivial and relaxed riverside country pub with model train often chugging around the bar, well kept real ales, spiral stairs to roomy additional upper dining area, good fresh food with more attention to vegetarian cooking than

is usual up here and plenty of fresh local produce; tables outside, self-catering flat

Free house ~ Licensee Wilson Forbes ~ Real ale ~ Bar food (12–2, 5.30–9; 12–2.30, 5–9.30 Sat, Sun) ~ (01339) 886137 ~ Children welcome ~ Dogs allowed in bar ~ Open 11–2.30, 5–11(12 Fri); 11–11(12 Sat) Sun; closed 25 Dec, 26 Dec evening, 1–3 Jan

ARDFERN

Galley of Lorne *B8002; village and inn signposted off A816 Lochgilphead–Oban*

Lively and welcoming, just across from Loch Craignish, with a warming log fire, an unfussy assortment of furniture, and good interesting home-made bar food; seats out on the sheltered terrace have marvellously peaceful views of the sea, loch and yacht anchorage; very good breakfasts

Free house ~ Licensee John Dobbie ~ Real ale ~ Bar food (12–2.30, 6–8.30) ~ Restaurant ~ (01852) 500284 ~ Children welcome ~ Dogs allowed in bar and bedrooms ~ Open 12(11 Sat, Sun)–12; closed 3–5 wkdays winter; closed 25 Dec ~ Bedrooms: £45B/£70B

BADACHRO

Badachro Inn *2½ miles S of Gairloch village turn off A832 on to B8056, then after another 3½ miles turn right in Badachro to the quay and inn*

Convivial inn in delightful waterside setting, charming local atmosphere in bar, dining conservatory, huge log fires, good food; Casper the pub spaniel is friendly, the terrace virtually overhangs the water, and the quiet road comes to a dead end a few miles further on at the lovely Redpoint beach

Free house ~ Licensee Martyn Pearson ~ Real ale ~ Bar food (12–3, 6–9) ~ Restaurant ~ (01445) 741255 ~ Children welcome ~ Dogs allowed in bar ~ Open 12–12(11.30 Sat); 12.30–11 Sun; only 5–11(12.30–6 Sun) middle of winter

ELIE
Ship *The Toft, off A917 (High Street) towards harbour*
Welcoming seaside pub overlooking the broad sands and bay, partly panelled villagey beamed bar with buoyant nautical feel and coal fires, friendly staff, enjoyable bar food; shorefront terrace tables, occasional barbecues
Free house ~ Licensees Richard and Jill Philip ~ Real ale ~ Bar food ~ (01333) 330246 ~ Children in eating area of bar and restaurant ~ Dogs allowed in bar ~ Open 11–12(1 Fri, Sat); 12.30–12 Sun; 11–11(12 Fri, Sat) winter; closed 25 Dec ~ Bedrooms: £30B/£50B

GLENELG
Glenelg Inn *Unmarked road from Shiel Bridge (A87) towards Skye*
Super old inn with enthusiastic landlord and friendly staff, unspoilt bar with almost a mountain cabin feel – crates and fish boxes serve as extra seating; short range of good bar meals made from fresh local ingredients, outstanding four-course evening meals, good choice of malt whiskies, lovely views to Skye from the garden; excellent bedrooms (price includes dinner), and staff are helpful with walk suggestions
Free house ~ Licensee Christopher Main ~ Bar food (12–2, 6–9) ~ Restaurant ~ (01599) 522273 ~ Children welcome ~ Dogs allowed in bar and bedrooms ~ Ceilidh Sat evening ~ Open 12–2.30, 5–11; 12–2.30 Sun; closed Sun evening ~ Bedrooms: £79B/£158B

KINGHOLM QUAY
Swan *B726 just S of Dumfries; or signposted off B725*
Well cared-for small hotel in quiet spot overlooking the old fishing jetty, neat and comfortable public bar, reliably good food inc high teas in the well ordered lounge or at busy times in the restaurant, friendly service; tables out in a small

garden with a play area; we haven't yet heard from readers who have stayed in the bedrooms here, but this would be a handy base for the Caerlaverock nature reserve with its vast numbers of geese

Free house ~ Licensees Billy Holesky, Tracy Rogan, Jackie and Jim Gibson ~ Real ale ~ Bar food (12–2, 5–8.30) ~ (01387) 253756 ~ Children welcome ~ Dogs allowed in bar ~ Open 11.30–2.30, 5–11(12 Fri); 11.30–11 Sun; closed 25, 26 Dec, 1 Jan

KIPPFORD

Anchor *Off A710 S of Dalbeattie*

Busy waterfront inn, overlooking big natural harbour and peaceful hills beyond, traditional back bar, no smoking lounge bar more used for eating, decent generous bar food; good bedrooms with lovely views, and the surrounding countryside is good for walks and bird-watching

Free house ~ Licensee Jenny Young ~ Real ale ~ Bar food (12–2.30, 6–9(12–2, 6–8.30 in winter)) ~ (01556) 620205 ~ Children welcome ~ Dogs allowed in bar ~ Open 10.30–12; 11.30–3, 6–11(12 Sat, Sun) in winter; closed 25 Dec ~ Bedrooms: /£60B

PLOCKTON

Plockton Hotel *Village signposted from A87 near Kyle of Lochalsh*

Most enjoyable little hotel stunningly placed by lovely sea loch, mountains beyond; leather seats in welcoming tartan-carpeted lounge bar with panelling, model ships and stripped stone, separate games bar, very good promptly served bar food; garden tables, comfortable and attractive bedrooms, excellent breakfast

Free house ~ Licensee Tom Pearson ~ Real ale ~ Bar food (12–2.30, 6–9.30) ~ Restaurant ~ (01599) 544274 ~ Children in eating area of bar and restaurant ~ Dogs allowed in bar ~ Open 11–12(11.30 Sat); 12.30–11 Sun; closed 1 Jan ~ Bedrooms: £40B/£80B

PORTPATRICK
Crown *North Crescent*

Very appealing timeless hotel a stone's throw from the lively small harbour, with tables out in front, a rambling old-fashioned bar with welcoming obliging staff, good malt whiskies and wines, and good food especially fresh local seafood, also attractive early 20th-c restaurant; sheltered back garden, nice bedrooms, good breakfasts

Free house ~ Licensee Mr A Schofield ~ Bar food (12–10) ~ Restaurant ~ (01776) 810261 ~ Children in eating area of bar and restaurant ~ Dogs allowed in bar ~ Folk most Fridays ~ Open 11.30–12(1 Sat); 12–11.30 Sun ~ Bedrooms: £43B/£72B

SKEABOST
Skeabost House Hotel *A850 NW of Portree, 1½ miles past junction with A856*

Grand-looking hotel in 12 acres of secluded woodland and gardens (and 9-hole golf course), glorious views over Loch Snizort, high-ceilinged plush bar, fine panelled billiards room, separate public games bar, good drinks choice especially malt whiskies, enjoyable bar food from airy dining conservatory, smart main dining room; comfortable and attractive bedrooms, excellent breakfast

Free house ~ Licensee Michael John Heaney ~ Real ale ~ Bar food (12–2, 6.30–9) ~ Restaurant ~ (01470) 532202 ~ Children in family room and over-13s in restaurant ~ Dogs allowed in bar and bedrooms ~ Open 12–2, 6–11; 12–11 Sun ~ Bedrooms: £47B/£80B

STEIN
Stein Inn *End of B886 N of Dunvegan in Waternish, off A850 Dunvegan–Portree; OS Sheet 23, map reference 263564*

Warmly welcoming 18th-c inn in perfect tranquil setting just above a quiet sea inlet, tables out looking over the sea to the Hebrides; fine choice of malt whiskies and real ale, character beamed and flagstoned public bar with peat fire, comfortable no smoking lounge and dining area, good value enjoyable bar food using local fish and Highland meat, good service; small inside play area; we have not yet had reports on the recently done bedrooms

Free house ~ Licensees Angus and Teresa McGhie ~ Real ale ~ Bar food (12–4, 6–9.30; no food in winter except Fri evenings (though food available for residents then)) ~ Restaurant ~ (01470) 592362 ~ Children welcome ~ Dogs welcome ~ Open 11–midnight(1am Fri, 12.30am Sat); 12.30–11 Sun; 4–11(midnight Fri); 12–12.30 Sat; 12.30–11 Sun winter; closed 25 Dec, 1 Jan ~ Bedrooms: £24.50B/£49B

TUSHIELAW

Tushielaw Inn *Ettrick Valley, B709/B7009 Lockerbie–Selkirk*
Friendly inn by Ettrick Water, enjoyable food inc good Galloway beef, unpretentious and comfortable little bar with open fire, local prints and photographs, and several antiques; tables out on terrace, and the inn has its own fishing on Clearburn Loch up the B711

Free house ~ Licensee Gordon Harrison ~ Real ale ~ Bar food ~ Restaurant ~ (01750) 62205 ~ Children welcome ~ Dogs welcome ~ Open 12–2.30, 6.30–11(7–10.30 Sun); cl Mon–Weds in winter ~ Bedrooms: £25B/£50B

WEEM

Ailean Chraggan *B846*
Two outside terraces at this family-run hotel enjoy a lovely view to the mountains beyond the Tay, sweeping up to Ben Lawers (the highest in this part of Scotland). Small and welcoming, it is an enjoyable place to stay, with good food, and chatty locals in the bar. Breakfasts are hearty, and dogs can stay too, but must have their own bedding. Good food in comfortably carpeted modern lounge or mainly no

smoking dining room, very good wine list, around 100 malt whiskies

Free house ~ Licensee Alastair Gillespie ~ Bar food ~ Restaurant ~ (01887) 820346 ~ Children welcome ~ Dogs allowed in bar and bedrooms ~ Open 11–11; closed 25–26 Dec, 1–2 Jan ~ Bedrooms: £42.50B/£85B

WALES
MID WALES

Dog Friendly Hotels and B&Bs

ABERDOVEY Penhelig Arms *Terrace Rd, Aberdovey, Gwynedd LL35 0LT (01654) 767215* **£80***, plus special breaks; 14 comfortable rms, 4 impressively furnished rooms in annexe with fine harbour views. Carefully refurbished building in fine spot overlooking sea, with cosy bar, open fires, delicious food with emphasis on daily-delivered fresh local fish in no smoking restaurant, extensive (and fairly priced) wine list with 14 by the glass (champagne, too), splendid breakfasts, and charming friendly service; lovely views of Dovey estuary; cl 25–26 Dec; dogs welcome in bedrooms

CRICKHOWELL Bear *High St, Crickhowell, Powys NP8 1BW (01873) 810408* **£70**; 35 rms, the back ones are the best, and some have jacuzzis. Particularly friendly coaching inn with calmly civilised atmosphere, excellent food using local produce and home-grown herbs (some Welsh specialities), fine wines and ports, well kept real ales, and prompt attentive service; lots of antiques, deeply comfortable seats, and a roaring log fire in the heavily beamed lounge, and a partly no smoking family room; children over 5 in restaurant; dogs welcome except in dining room

EGLWYSFACH Ynyshir Hall *Eglwysfach, Machynlleth, Dyfed SY20 8TA (01654) 781209* **£160***, plus special breaks; 9 individually decorated, no smoking rms, two with four-posters. Carefully run Georgian manor house in 14 acres of landscaped gardens adjoining the Ynyshir coastal bird reserve, with particularly good service, antiques, log fires and paintings in the light and airy public rooms, extremely good food using home-grown vegetables, and delicious breakfasts; lots to do nearby; cl 3 wks Jan; children over 9; disabled access to ground floor rms; dogs welcome in bedrooms

LLANGAMMARCH WELLS Lake *Llangammarch Wells, Powys LD4 4BS (01591) 620202* **£170***, plus special breaks; 19 charming, pretty rms with fruit and decanter of sherry. Particularly well run 1860 half-timbered hotel in 50 acres with plenty of wildlife, well stocked trout lake, clay pigeon shoots, tennis, and riding or walk their two friendly Labradors; deeply comfortable tranquil drawing room with antiques, paintings and log fire, wonderful afternoon teas (in summer under the chestnut tree overlooking the river), courteous discreet service, fine wines and very good modern British cooking in elegant candlelit dining room, and liberal breakfasts; children over 7 in evening dining room; disabled access; dogs welcome in bedrooms

LLANWRTYD WELLS Carlton House *Dolycoed Rd, Llanwrtyd Wells, Powys LD5 4RA (01591) 610248* **£65***, plus special breaks; 7 well equipped rms. Warmly friendly owners run this comfortable Edwardian restaurant-with-rooms, and there's a relaxing little sitting room with plants and antiques, an attractive dining room with original panelling and log fire, exceptionally good modern British cooking using top-quality local produce (delicious puddings and home-made canapés and petits fours), super breakfasts with home-made bread and marmalade, and a thoughtful wine list; cl 10–28 Dec; dogs welcome in bedrooms

MONTGOMERY Dragon *Market Sq, Montgomery, Powys SY15 6PA (01686) 668359* **£75**, plus special breaks; 20 rms. Attractive black and white timbered small hotel with a pleasant grey-stone tiled hall, comfortable residents' lounge, beamed bar, restaurant using local produce; indoor swimming pool, sauna; dogs welcome in bedrooms

PRESTEIGNE Radnorshire Arms *High St, Presteigne, Powys LD8 2BE (01544) 267406* **£82**; 16 rms. Rambling handsomely timbered 17th-c hotel with old-fashioned charm and an unchanging atmosphere, elegantly moulded beams and fine dark panelling in the lounge bar, latticed windows, enjoyable food (inc morning coffee and afternoon tea), separate no smoking restaurant, well kept real ales, and politely attentive service; dogs welcome

RHAYADER Beili Neuadd *Rhayader, Powys LD6 5NS (01597) 810211* **£47***; 3 rms with log fires, and newly converted stone barn with 3 bunkhouse rms. Charming partly 16th-c stone-built farmhouse in quiet countryside (they have their own trout pools and woodland), with beams, polished oak floorboards, and nice breakfasts in new garden room; self-catering also; cl Christmas; children over 8; dogs welcome in bedrooms

NORTH WALES

Dog Friendly Hotels and B&Bs

ABERSOCH Porth Tocyn Hotel *Bwlch Tocyn, Pwllheli, Gwynedd LL53 7BU (01758) 713303* **£102**, plus special breaks; 17 attractive rms, most with sea views. On a headland overlooking Cardigan Bay, a lovely place to stay – with a refreshingly sensible and helpful approach to families (though not solely a family hotel) – and carefully refurbished this year; very friendly hard-working owners and staff, several cosy interconnecting sitting rooms with antiques and fresh flowers, most enjoyable traditional cooking in the restaurant (lots of options such as light lunches, high teas for children (as they must be over 7 for dinner in the restaurant), and imaginative Sun lunches), and a happy atmosphere; lots of space in the pretty garden, heated swimming pool in summer, hard tennis court; cl mid-Nov to mid-Mar; disabled access; dogs welcome in bedrooms

BEDDGELERT Sygun Fawr Country House *Beddgelert, Caernarfon, Gwynedd LL55 4NE (01766) 890258* **£64**, plus special breaks; 9 rms. Spectacular scenery surrounds this secluded 17th-c hotel, with lots of surrounding walks; beams, stripped stone walls, inglenooks, and a restful atmosphere, a varied imaginative menu, antiques and an informal atmosphere in the restaurant, and 20 acres of mountainside and gardens; cl Jan; dogs welcome in bedrooms

BETWS-Y-COED Ty Gwyn *Betws-y-Coed, Gwynedd LL24 0SG (01690) 710383* **£56**, plus special breaks; 12 pretty rms, most with own bthrm. Welcoming and well run 17th-c coaching inn with interesting old prints, furniture and bric-a-brac, good food and friendly service; pleasant setting overlooking river and a very good base for the area; children free if sharing parents' room; cl Mon–Weds in Jan; disabled access; dogs welcome in bedrooms

CAERNARFON Seiont Manor *Llanrug, Caernarfon, Gwynedd LL55 2AQ (01286) 673366* **£140**, plus special breaks; 28 luxurious rms. Fine hotel built from the original farmstead of a Georgian manor house, in 156 acres of mature parkland; open fires and comfortable sofas in lounge, restful atmosphere in library and drawing room, imaginative food in restaurant's four interconnecting areas, and leisure suite with swimming pool, gym, and sauna; dogs welcome in bedrooms

CONWY Sychnant Pass House *Sychnant Pass Rd, Conwy, Gwynedd LL32 8BJ (01492) 596868* **£70***; 10 rms. Victorian house in two acres among the foothills of the Snowdonia National Park; big comfortable sitting rooms, log fires, a relaxing, friendly atmosphere, and enjoyable food (the restaurant is open to non-residents, too); cl late Dec–Jan; disabled access; dogs welcome

GELLILYDAN Tyddyn Du Farm *Gellilydan, Blaenau Ffestiniog, Gwynedd LL41 4RB (01766) 590281* **£58***; 4 ground floor, private stable and long barn suites with jacuzzi baths, fridges and microwaves, one with airbath. 400-year-old farmhouse on working farm in the heart of Snowdonia, with beams and exposed stonework, big inglenook fireplaces in residents' lounge, and delicious candlelit evening meals; children can help with the lambs, goats, ducks, sheep and pony; fine walks, inc short one to their own Roman site; partial disabled access; dogs welcome

LLANABER Llwyndu Farmhouse *Llanaber, Barmouth, Gwynedd LL42 1RR (01341) 280144* **£64***, plus special breaks; 7 charming rms, most with own bthrm, some in a nicely converted 18th-c barn. Most attractive 16th-c farmhouse just above Cardigan Bay, with a warm welcome from friendly owners, big inglenook fireplaces, oak beams, little mullioned windows, relaxing lounge, enjoyable breakfasts, and good imaginative food in candlelit dining room; cl 25–26 Dec; dogs welcome in bedrooms

LLANARMON D C West Arms *Llanarmon Dyffryn Ceiriog, Llangollen, Clwyd LL20 7LD (01691) 600665* **£108***, plus special midweek breaks; 15 rms. Charming and civilised 16th-c inn with heavy beams and timbers, log fires in inglenook fireplaces, lounge bar interestingly furnished with antique settles, sofas in the old-fashioned entrance hall, comfortable locals' bar, good food, and friendly quiet atmosphere; the lawn runs down to the River Ceiriog (fishing for residents); disabled access; dogs welcome away from restaurant

LLANDRILLO Tyddyn Llan *Llandrillo, Corwen, Clwyd LL21 0ST (01490) 440264* **£105**; 10 pretty rms. Restful Georgian house with fresh flowers and antiques in elegantly furnished and comfortable public rooms, charming staff, very good inventive food (using their own herbs) and three acres of lovely gardens; fishing on four miles of River Dee (ghillies available) and fine forest walks (guides available) – can arrange riding and shooting too; cl 2 wks Jan; dogs welcome in bedrooms

LLANFAIR D C Eyarth Station *Llanfair Dyffryn Clwyd, Ruthin, Clwyd LL15 2EE (01824) 703643* **£48***, plus special breaks; 6 pretty rms. Carefully converted old railway station with quiet gardens and wonderful views, a friendly relaxed atmosphere, log fire in airy and comfortable beamed lounge, good breakfasts and enjoyable suppers in dining room (more lovely views), sun terrace and heated swimming pool, and lots of walks; cl Jan–Feb; disabled access; dogs welcome in bedrooms

LLANSANFFRAID GLAN CONWY Old Rectory Country House *Llanrwst Rd, Glan Conwy, Colwyn Bay, Clwyd LL28 5LF (01492) 580611* **£199** inc dinner, plus special breaks; 6 deeply comfortable rms. Georgian house in pleasant gardens with fine views over Conwy estuary, Conwy Castle and Snowdonia; delightful public rms with flowers, antiques and family photos, delicious food of the highest restaurant standards, and marvellous wines; good breakfasts, warmly friendly staff; cl Dec–Jan, open wknd only Nov and Feb; children under 9 months or over 5; dogs in coach house only

LLANWDDYN Lake Vyrnwy Hotel *Llanwddyn, Oswestry, Powys SY10 0LY (01691) 870692* **£115**; 35 rms, the ones overlooking the lake are the nicest – and quietest. Large impressive Tudor-style mansion overlooking lake from hillside in 40 square miles of forestry, with lots of sporting activities (esp fishing), log fires and sporting prints in the comfortable and elegant public rooms, relaxed atmosphere, bar, and good food using home-made preserves, chutneys, mustards and vinegars and produce from own kitchen garden; enjoyable teas too; dogs welcome in bedrooms

NANTGWYNANT   Pen-y-Gwryd *Nantgwynant, Caernarfon, Gwynedd LL55 4NT (01286) 870211* **£62***, plus special breaks; 16 rms, some with own bthrm. In two acres, this cheery hotel is by the Llanberis Pass in Snowdonia National Park; warm log fire in simply furnished panelled residents' lounge, rugged slate-floored bar that doubles as mountain rescue post; lots of climbing mementoes and equipment, friendly, chatty games room (lots of walkers, climbers and fishermen), hearty enjoyable food, big breakfasts, and packed lunches; sauna in the trees and outdoor swimming pool, table tennis; private chapel; cl Nov–New Year and midweek Jan–Feb; disabled access; dogs welcome away from dining room

TAL-Y-BONT Lodge *Tal-y-bont, Conwy, Gwynedd LL32 8YX (01492) 660766* **£72**, plus special breaks; 14 rms. Friendly little modern hotel in over three acres on the edge of Snowdonia, with open fire, books and magazines in comfortable lounge, generous helpings of popular food using lots of home-grown produce in no smoking restaurant, and good service; lots of walks; well behaved pets welcome; good disabled access; dogs welcome in bedrooms

TALSARNAU Maes-y-Neuadd *Talsarnau, Gwynedd LL47 6YA (01766) 780200* **£143*** inc 4-course dinner, plus special breaks; 16 luxurious rms. Looking out across Snowdonia, this attractive extended 14th-c mansion stands in eight acres of landscaped hillside; flowers, plants, antiques and open fires, peaceful atmosphere, very good food (herbs and vegetables from their own garden), friendly cats, and charming staff; disabled access; dogs welcome in bedrooms

South Wales

Dog Friendly Hotels and B&Bs

GILWERN Wenallt Farm *Twyn-wenallt, Gilwern, Abergavenny, Gwent NP7 0HP (01873) 830694* **£48***; 8 rms. Friendly and relaxing 16th-c Welsh longhouse on 50 acres of farmland, with oak beams and inglenook fireplace in big drawing room, a TV room, good food in dining room, and lots to do nearby; cl Christmas; dogs welcome in bedrooms

GOVILON Llanwenarth House *Govilon, Abergavenny, Gwent NP7 9SF (01873) 830289* **£86***, plus special breaks; 5 spacious, comfortable rms. Fine family-run 16th-c manor house in quiet grounds, with gracious sitting room, log fires, antiques and fresh flowers, fine food using local game and fish and home-produced meat, poultry and garden veg in elegant candlelit no smoking dining room, and friendly helpful staff; lots to do nearby; croquet; children over 10; disabled access; dogs welcome in bedrooms

MONMOUTH Riverside Hotel *Cinderhill St, Monmouth, Gwent NP25 5EY (01600) 715577* **£68**, plus special breaks; 17 rms. Comfortable, warmly welcoming bustling hotel overlooking River Monnow and the 13th-c fortified gatehouse, with good value bar meals, extensive restaurant menu, a bustling lounge, and conservatory; disabled access; dogs welcome in bedrooms

TINTERN PARVA Parva Farmhouse Hotel *Tintern, Chepstow, Gwent NP16 6SQ (01291) 689411* **£74***, plus special breaks; 9 comfortable rms. Friendly stone farmhouse built in 17th c, with leather chesterfields, woodburner and honesty bar in large beamed lounge, books (no TV downstairs), and very good food and wine (inc wine using locally grown grapes) in cosy restaurant; 50 yds from River Wye and lovely surrounding countryside; dogs welcome in bedrooms

WHITEBROOK Crown at Whitebrook *Whitebrook, Monmouth, Gwent NP25 4TX (01600) 860254* **£90***, plus special breaks; 10 neat rms. Small modernised restaurant-with-rooms in beautiful Wye Valley, with friendly caring service, relaxed atmosphere, comfortable lounge and bar;

small cosy restaurant with fine wines and excellent food combining Welsh ingredients and French style, very good breakfasts; cl 2 wks Christmas and New Year; children over 12; dogs welcome in bedrooms

WEST WALES

Dog Friendly Hotels and B&Bs

BROAD HAVEN Druidstone Hotel *Broad Haven, Haverfordwest, Dyfed SA62 3NE (01437) 781221* **£90***; 11 rms, some with sea view, shared bthrms. Alone on the coast above an effectively private beach with exhilarating cliff walks, this roomy and very informally friendly hotel, run by a very nice family, has something of a folk-club and Outward Bound feel at times; it's extremely winning and relaxing if you take to its unique combination of good wholesome and often memorably inventive food, slightly fend-for-yourself approach amid elderly furniture, and glorious seaside surroundings; self-catering cottages, two with wheelchair access; disabled access; dogs welcome

CRUGYBAR Glanrannell Park *Crugybar, Llanwrda, Dyfed SA19 8SA (01558) 685230* **£90***; 7 rms. Surrounded by lawns and overlooking a small private lake, this peaceful hotel has two comfortable lounges and a small library, a well stocked bar, good varied food using fresh local produce where possible, and friendly helpful staff; excellent area for walks and esp bird-watching, also lots of wildlife, pony-trekking, and fishing nearby; cl Nov–Mar; children over 8; dogs welcome in bedrooms

FISHGUARD Manor House Hotel *Main St, Fishguard, Dyfed SA65 9HG (01348) 873260* **£55***, plus special breaks;

6 comfortable rms, most with sea views. Georgian house with fine views of harbour from sheltered garden, a guests' lounge with books, an attractive, well planned basement restaurant with delicious home-made food using fresh local produce, and enjoyable breakfasts (and pre-dinner drinks), out on the terrace overlooking the sea in good weather; cl Christmas, Nov and part Jan; dogs welcome in bedrooms

GLYNARTHEN Penbontbren Farm *Glynarthen, Llandysul, Dyfed SA44 6PE (01239) 810248* **£86**, plus special breaks; 10 rms in converted stone farm outbuildings. Victorian farmhouse in lovely countryside with a little farm museum, and nearby beaches; period pine furnishings in bar, lounge and well liked restaurant, good honest country cooking and hearty breakfasts; cl 24–28 Dec; disabled access; dogs welcome in bedrooms

LLANDELOY Lochmeyler Farm *Llandeloy, Haverford-west, Dyfed SA62 6LL (01348) 837724* **£40***, plus special winter breaks; 15 pretty rms with videos (they have a video library). Attractive creeper-covered 16th-c farmhouse on 220-acre working dairy farm; two lounges (one no smoking), log fires, traditional farmhouse cooking in pleasant dining room, mature garden, and Welsh cakes on arrival; can walk around the farm trails; cl Christmas and New Year; disabled access; dogs welcome in bedrooms

SPITTAL Lower Haythog *Spittal, Haverfordwest, Dyfed SA62 5QL (01437) 731279* **£50**; 6 rms. Centuries-old farmhouse on working dairy farm in 250 acres of unspoilt countryside, with comfortable lounge, log fire, books and games, traditional breakfasts, good cooking in the dining room, and friendly owners; swing and slide in the garden, trout ponds in the woods; self-catering also; dogs welcome in bedrooms

ST DAVID'S Warpool Court *St David's, Haverfordwest, Dyfed SA62 6BN (01437) 720300* **£140***, plus special breaks; 25 rms. Originally built as St David's cathedral school in the 1860s and bordering NT land, this popular hotel has lovely views over St Bride's Bay; Ada Williams's collection of lovely hand-painted tiles can be seen in the public rooms, food in the spacious elegant restaurant is imaginative (good for vegetarians too), and staff are helpful and friendly; quiet gardens, heated summer swimming pool, tennis, exercise room, table-tennis, pool and croquet; cl Jan; dogs welcome in bedrooms

Dog Friendly Pubs

ABERGORLECH
Black Lion *B4310 (a pretty road roughly NE of Carmarthen)*
Welcoming little 17th-c coaching inn in the beautiful Cothi Valley, with the Brechfa Forest around it and lots of good walks nearby; stripped stone and flagstones, black beams, high-backed settles, good value bar food and summer afternoon teas, cheerful service, sociable springer spaniel called Toby; garden slopes down towards the river
Free house ~ Licensee Jean de Russett ~ Bar food (12–2.30(3 Sun), 7–9; not Mon, not evening Sun) ~ (01558) 685271 ~ Children welcome away from bar ~ Dogs welcome ~ Open 12–3.30, 7–11; 12–5, 7–(10.30 Sun)11 Sat; closed Mon except bank hols and evening Sun

BERRIEW
Lion *B4390; village signposted off A483 Welshpool–Newtown*
Country inn in pretty riverside village not far from Powis Castle, with nicely old-fashioned black-beamed public bar,

good photographs in comfortable lounge bar, wood fires, enjoyable food (only roasts on Sun), friendly efficient staff; we have not yet heard from readers who have stayed in the chintzy bedrooms

Free house ~ Licensees Tim Woodward and Sue Barton ~ Bar food (not Sun evening) ~ Restaurant ~ (01686) 640452 ~ Children welcome away from main bar ~ Dogs allowed in bar and bedrooms ~ Open 12–3, 6–11; 12–3, 7–(10.30 Sun)11 Sat ~ Bedrooms: £55S(£55B)/£70S(£70B)

LLANBERIS

Pen-y-Gwryd *Nant Gwynant; at junction of A498 and A4086, ie across mountains from Llanberis – OS Sheet 115, map reference 660558*

High in Snowdonia, a great favourite with mountaineers for generations (it still doubles as a mountain rescue post); homely slate-floored log cabin bar, smaller room with illustrious boots from famous climbs, more climbing mementoes in cosy panelled smoke room, hearty lunchtime home cooking, very friendly staff, good drinks; a nice place to stay

Free house ~ Licensee Jane Pullee ~ Real ale ~ Bar food (lunchtime) ~ Restaurant (evening) ~ No credit cards ~ (01286) 870211 ~ Children welcome ~ Dogs allowed in bar and bedrooms ~ Open 11–11(10.30 Sun); closed Nov–Dec, Mon–Thurs Jan–Feb ~ Bedrooms: £26/£52(£62S)(£62B)

LLANFERRES

Druid *A494 Mold–Ruthin*

17th-c inn with valley and mountain views, civilised plush lounge and bigger beamed back bar, attractive dining area, welcoming staff, wide range of generous changing bar food inc lots of daily fresh fish; tables outside, comfortable bedrooms

Burtonwood ~ Tenant James Dolan ~ Real ale ~ Bar food

(12–2.30, 6–9.30; all day Sat, Sun and bank hols) ~ Restaurant ~ (01352) 810225 ~ Children welcome ~ Dogs allowed in bar and bedrooms ~ Welsh sing-along first Sat of month ~ Open 12–3, 5.30–11; 12–11 Sat and bank hols; 12–10.30 Sun ~ Bedrooms: £28.50(£35B)/£38.50(£60S)(£48.50B)

LLANGYNIDR

Coach & Horses *Cwm Crawnon Road (B4558 W of Crickhowell)*

Winter walkers appreciate the large open fire at this old coaching inn, with comfortable banquettes against stripped stone walls, a handy choice of generous bar food, or restaurant dishes; well fenced lawn running down to the Newport & Brecon Canal, comfortable bedrooms

Free house ~ Licensee Derek Latham ~ Real ale ~ Bar food (12–2, 6.30–9.30) ~ Restaurant ~ (01874) 730245 ~ Children in eating area of bar and restaurant ~ Dogs allowed in bar and bedrooms ~ Open 11–11; 12–10.30 Sun ~ Bedrooms: £22.50(£28.50B)/£40(£50B)

PONTYPOOL

Open Hearth *The Wern, Griffithstown; Griffithstown signposted off A4051 S – opposite main works entrance turn up hill, then first right*

Good real ale choice, lots of malt whiskies, decent wines and home-made food, comfortably modernised smallish lounge bar with big stone fireplace, second back bar, seats outside overlook overgrown stretch of Monmouthshire & Brecon Canal, adventure play area

Enterprise ~ Lease John and Emma Bennett ~ Real ale ~ Bar food (11.30–2, 6.30–10) ~ Restaurant ~ (01495) 763752 ~ Children away from main bar ~ Dogs allowed in bar ~ Open 11.30–11; 12–10.30 Sun

MAPS

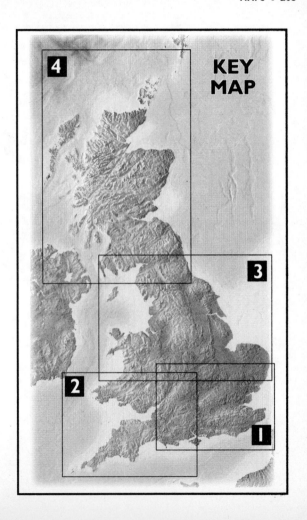

KEY
MAP

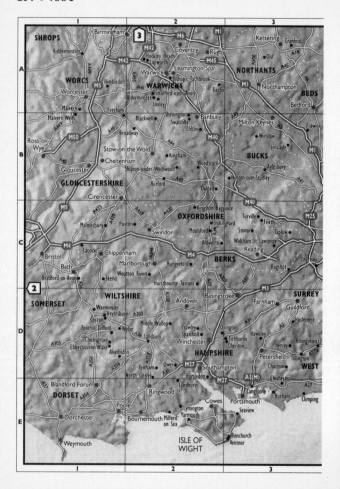

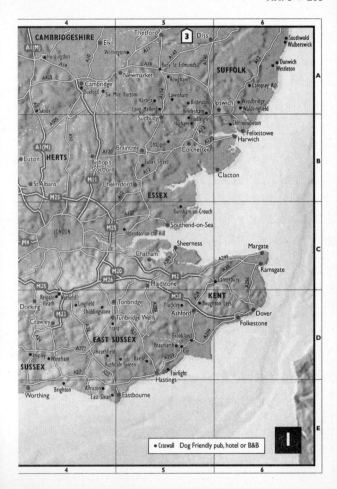

Craswall Dog Friendly pub, hotel or B&B

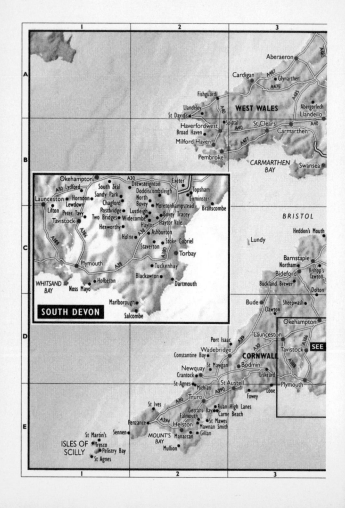

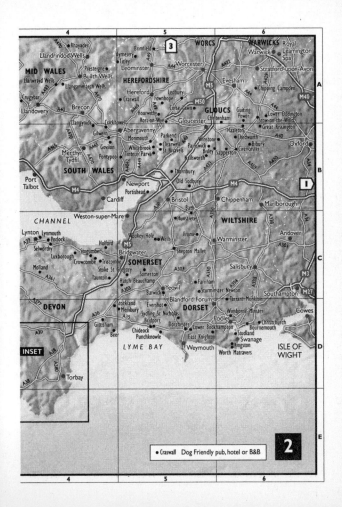

MID WALES · Rhayader · Llandrindod Wells · Presteigne · Builth Wells · Llanwrtyd Wells · Llangammarch Wells · Crugybar · Brecon · Llandovery · Llangynidr · Crickhowell · Gilwern · Merthyr Tydfil · Govilon · Pontypool · Whitebrook · Tintern Parva · **SOUTH WALES** · Port Talbot · Newport · Portishead · Cardiff

HEREFORDSHIRE · Brimfield · Lyonshall · Titley · Leominster · Worcester · **WORCS** · Hereford · Craswall · Fownhope · Ledbury · Hoarwithy · Corse Lawn · Ross-on-Wye · Abergavenny · Monmouth · Parkend · Clearwell · St Bravels · **GLOUCS** · Gloucester · Cheltenham · Winstone · Painswick · Bisley · Sapperton · Nailsworth · Thornbury · Old Sodbury · Bristol · Barn · **WARWICKS** · Royal Leamington Spa · Warwick · Stratford-upon-Avon · Chipping Campden · Evesham · Guiting Power · Lower Oddington · Stow-on-the-Wold · Great Rissington · Hazleton · Chedworth · Bibury · Cirencester · Oxford

3

M5 · M50 · M40 · M4 · M5

WILTSHIRE · Humstrete · Frome · Warminster · Andover · Wookey Hole · Wells · Shepton Mallet · **SOMERSET** · Bridgwater · Somerton · Yeovil · Farnham · Sturminster Newton · Salisbury · Southampton · Cowes · Chippenham · Marlborough · Chipstable

CHANNEL · Weston-super-Mare · Lynton · Lynmouth · Porlock · Selworthy · Holford · Stogumber · Luxborough · Crowcombe · Triscombe · Molland · Stoke St Gregory · Taunton · Hatch Beauchamp · Barwick · **DEVON** · Stockland · Membury · Eversholt · Sydling St Nicholas · Blandford Forum · **DORSET** · Tarrant Monkton · Wimborne Minster · Poole · Christchurch · Bournemouth · Gittisham · Bridport · Chideock · Punchknowle · Dorchester · Lower Bockhampton · East Knighton · Studland · **ISLE OF WIGHT** · Beer · **LYME BAY** · Weymouth · Worth Matravers · Kingston · Swanage

INSET · Torbay

2

• Craswall   Dog Friendly pub, hotel or B&B

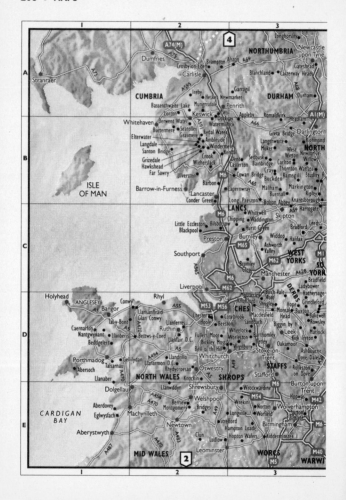

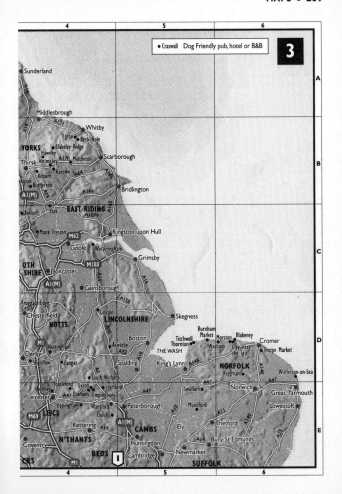

● Craswall   Dog Friendly pub, hotel or B&B

3

● Sunderland

A

Middlesbrough
Whitby
Egton ● Beck Hole
YORKS   Blakeley Ridge
Hawnby   A170   Middleton   Scarborough
Thirsk Helmsley
Harome   A64
Kilburn
Ripon Brafferton

B

A166   Bridlington

Linton   Tork
EAST RIDING
AJ079

● Monk Fryston   M62   Kingston upon Hull
Goole   Winteringham

UTH
SHIRE   Doncaster   M180   Grimsby

A1(M)
Gainsborough

C

Froggatt Edge
Litton   Lincoln
Chesterfield   Skegness
NOTTS   LINCOLNSHIRE
Burnham
M1   Market   Blakeney
Boston   Titchwell   Morston
Nottingham   Thornton   Cromer
Derby   Ancaster   A52   Waxham   Cley-next-   Thorpe Market
Shardlow   Langar   THE WASH   the sea
South Witham   Spalding   King's Lynn   A149
Stapleford   Exton   Stamford   NORFOLK   Winterton-on-Sea
Leicester   A47 Oakham Empingham   A47   Reepham   A47
Uppingham Wansford   Swaffam   Norwich   Great Yarmouth
LEICS   Oundle   Peterborough   Lowestoft
Kettering   A14   A1(M)   Mundford
N'THANTS   CAMBS   Ely   Thetford
Coventry   Huntingdon   A14   Bury St Edmunds
BEDS   Cambridge   Newmarket
CKS   M1   SUFFOLK

D

E

4   5   6

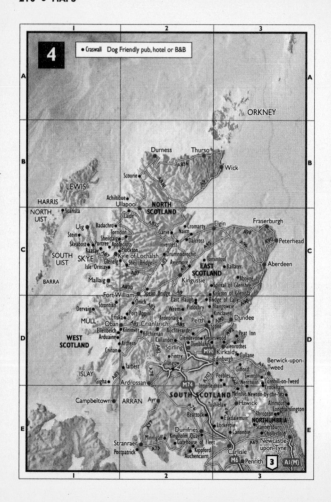

4 • Craswall Dog Friendly pub, hotel or B&B

ORKNEY

Durness Thurso
Wick
Scourie

LEWIS

HARRIS
Achiltibue
Ullapool
NORTH UIST Scansta NORTH SCOTLAND
Laide
Uig Badachro A835
Stein Torridon Cromarty
Skeabost Sheildaig Garve Nairn Elgin Fraserburgh
Raasay Portree Applecross Inverness Dalcross Peterhead
SOUTH UIST Plockton Kyle of Lochalsh Drumnadrochit A98
SKYE Glenelg Sheil Bridge Aviemore Tomintoul EAST SCOTLAND Aberdeen
Isle Ornsay A87 Ballater
BARRA Mallaig Kingussie Aboyne
Fort William Spean Bridge Spittal of Glenshee
Kirkton of Glenisla
Dervaig Strontian Onich East Haugh Bridge of Cally
Erska Port Appin Weem Pitlochry Blairgowrie
MULL Ellenbeich Oban Ardeonaig Perth Kinclaven
WEST Arduaine Kilchrenan Callander Scone Dundee
SCOTLAND Ardfern Crianlarich Glendevone Kingswood Peat Inn
Eniton Kilmore Auchterarder Elie
Stirling Dunblane Glenrothes
Fintry M90 Kirkcaldy
Tarbert Glasgow Edinburgh Gullane
ISLAY Peebles Gifford Berwick-upon-Tweed
Gigha Ardrossan Innerleithen Swinton Cornhill-on-Tweed
SOUTH SCOTLAND Nenthorn Fogo
Campbeltown ARRAN Ayr Melrose Newton-by-the-Sea
Tushielaw Hawick Alnmouth
Beattock Longframlington
Eskdalemuir Shropton NORTHUMBRIA
Dumfries Lockerbie Stannersburn
Minnigaff Kingholm Quay Canonbie Chollerford
Stranraer Gatehouse of Fleet Uppford A69 Newcastle-upon-Tyne
Portpatrick Auchencairn Carlisle
M6 Penrith **3** A1(M)

Also available from Ebury:

The Good Pub Guide
Ed. Alisdair Aird

'Easily the best national pub guide' *Time Out*
'*The Good Pub Guide* lives in my glove compartment' *Sunday Times*

The number one bestselling UK guide book. With over 5,000 entries the *Good Pub Guide* is 100% independent, honest and comprehensive. With awards for food, beer, wine, whisky and many more, Alisdair Aird will take you to the finest pubs in the land.

The Good Britain Guide
Ed Alisdair Aird

'An exceptional guide' *Sunday Telegraph*

Uniquely honest, detailed and wide-ranging, *The Good Britain Guide* will lead you and your family to the best of British. From seaside holidays with toddlers to days out with teenagers, from weekends away with friends or a city-break with your partner, *The Good Britain Guide* lists the best places to eat, stay and visit.

The Good Hotel Guide – UK & Ireland
Ed Caroline Raphael and Desmond Balmer

'The one guide that offers a sense of what a hotel is really like' *Mail*

In its 26 years of reporting *The Good Hotel Guide* has become a byword for accurate, evocative and insightful reporting. The totally independent guide covers over 750 hotels from charming, small b&bs to lavish country house hotels.

The Good Hotel Guide – Continental Europe
Ed Adam and Caroline Raphael

'I cannot imagine a visit to the continent without this splendid guide.' Simon Jenkins, *The Times*
'Not only highly useful but a very good read.' Sue MacGregor

A uniquely honest and descriptive guide to the finest hotels and b&bs in Europe. Acclaimed year after year for its style, reliability and wide selection of characterful, comfortable places to stay.

Pocket Good Guide to Great Food Pubs
Pocket Good Guide to Great Family Days Out
Pocket Good Guide to Historic Britain
Ed Alisdair Aird

All Ebury titles are available in good bookshops or via mail order

TO ORDER
(please tick)

Pocket Good Guide to Great Food Pubs	£5.99
Pocket Good Guide to Great Family Days Out	£5.99
Pocket Good Guide to Historic Britain	£5.99
The Good Pub Guide	£14.99
The Good Britain Guide	£14.99
The Good Hotel Guide to UK and Ireland	£15.99
The Good Hotel Guide to Continental Europe	£16.99

PAYMENT MAY BE MADE USING ACCESS, VISA, MASTERCARD, DINERS CLUB, SWITCH AND AMEX OR CHEQUE, EUROCHEQUE AND POSTAL ORDER (STERLING ONLY)

CARD NUMBER:

EXPIRY DATE:............   SWITCH ISSUE NO:.................

SIGNATURE:...

PLASE ALLOW £2.50 FOR POST AND PACKAGING FOR THE FIRST BOOK AND £1.00 THEREAFTER

ORDER TOTAL: £   (INC P&P)

ALL ORDERS TO:

EBURY PRESS, BOOKS BY POST, TBS LIMITED, COLCHESTER ROAD, FRATING GREEN, COLCHESTER, ESSEX CO7 7DW, UK

TELEHONE: 01206 256 000
FAX: 01206 255 914

NAME:

ADDRESS:

Please allow 28 days for delivery. Please tick box if you do not wish to receive any additional information

Prices and availability subject to change without notice.